to have & to hold

to have & to hold

magical wedding bouquets

DAVID STARK AND AVI ADLER

WITH JOHN MORSE AND SUSAN MONTAGNA

PHOTOGRAPHS BY MICK HALES

ARTISAN

NEW YORK

Photographs copyright © 2005 by Mick Hales except for what follows.

Photographs by Philippe Cheng: pages 5, 6, 14, 16 (left and right),
28 (bottom), 38, 47 (top, right), 48 (right), 53, 78 (right), 80 (left),
104 (left), 124, 127, 130 (right), 134, 154, 178, 180, 187
Photographs by Kathy Litwin: pages 58, 204

Published by Artisan
A Division of Workman Publishing, Inc.
708 Broadway
New York, New York 10003-9555
www.artisanbooks.com

Library of Congress Cataloging-in-Publication Data is on file for this title.

ISBN-13: 978-1-57965-278-4
ISBN-10: 1-57965-278-6
LCCN: 2005045355

Printed in Singapore
10 9 8 7 6 5 4 3 2 1

Book design by Vivian Ghazarian and Mark Lerner

Contents

7   Introduction

13 Spring

77 Summer

129 Autumn

179 Winter

206 To Preserve and Protect Bouquets

207 Acknowledgments

Introduction

One of the sweetest moments of planning a wedding—
and we've been planning weddings of all sizes around the
globe for more than fourteen years—is the day we invite our
bride to join us for a little pre-wedding walk through the
flower market. Typically, it's on a day that follows months and
months of talking, planning, and designing "on paper."
It's a kick watching her excitement build as we stroll together
among countless bushels and carts of bountiful flowers,
pointing out the different species and detailing the benefits
and challenges of each one. Finally, after all the weeks and
months of talking about flowers and looking at pictures,
there we are, surrounded by the real thing.

The markets are feasts for the senses, a vast array of sumptuous, colorful blossoms, each with its own fragrance, texture, and composition. As we stroll, we clarify her likes and dislikes. "We're planning on these sunflowers for the church," we might offer, seeking her approval as we pass radiant buckets of Teddy Bears—and our bride gives a yes or no. Next, we single out, say, the fiery gloriosa daisies we'd discussed at length in the weeks before, thrilled that she can now match the face of this lustrous flower with its exotic name. You can almost hear the wheels turning as she starts to hone in on the various designs and combinations that will lead to a unique floral masterpiece. Time and again we've found our flower market "show and tell" to be the critical link in conceptualizing the ultimate bridal bouquet, and time and again brides have told us how important that market visit is to them.

If it's any comfort to the worried bride, she can at least be assured that she's not alone. Few elements of the wedding ritual are as ubiquitous as the bouquet. For as long as there have been weddings, brides have had flowers. From Polynesian women adorned in ambrosial leis to Indian brides showered in petals, from the most royal affair to getting hitched at city hall, the "I do" comes with flowers. Even a back-to-nature gal who marries barefoot on the beach in Malibu carries flowers. She may not have shoes, but you can bet she's got a bouquet.

Like the tradition of marriage itself, the history of the bouquet is a mosaic of traditions, cultures, and lore. In ancient Rome and Nordic cultures, young maidens clutched potent herbs as a way to bring luck and ward off evil spirits. In early Greece, brides chose ivy, a tenacious plant symbolizing a sturdy relationship. At about the same time, across the Mediterranean, the women of nomadic tribes in what is now Syria favored the fragrant blossoms of the orange tree, which has the uncommon ability to flower even as it bears fruit—a lovely metaphor for a happy marriage blessed with children.

Even the modern traditions associated with bouquets have ancient ties. The ritual tossing of the

A luscious array of lavenders and purples—scabiosas (also known as pincushion flowers), lisianthus, limoniums, lavender spray roses—is refreshed with interwoven Persian shield leaves and fragrant mint leaves (yes, the kind you eat)!

bouquet, for example, has its roots in a rather nasty bit of medieval revelry. Apparently, wedding ceremonies in the Middle Ages finished with the single men in attendance tearing at the garment of the bride in an effort to gain a souvenir that might bring them luck in landing lasses of their own. Among the most desired pieces of clothing was the garter, which the bride often tossed in hopes of avoiding the inconvenience of having it taken from her. Eventually, to make that ritual even safer, the groom took it upon himself to dispatch the garter to the eager bachelors, and the bride began to throw her flowers instead.

Over the centuries, the bouquet has been refined and reinterpreted in countless ways, becoming a fashion accessory every bit as important as jewelry or a veil. And as such, it is fraught with the same potential for success or failure: Will it be a floral gem that quietly speaks exquisite taste or a disappointing array that distracts from the bride's presence and sticks out forever in every wedding-day portrait? Too big, and

it hides the bride's shape and weighs her down. Too small, and it's lost in a sea of fabric, relegated to insignificance. Color, of course, is critical, but how do you tap the brightest colors of spring if your nuptials are slated for January and the closest florist is hundreds of miles away? What if the big day falls close to Thanksgiving, but the last thing you want is a bouquet that looks like a harvest cornucopia lifted from the holiday table? And what if you're a biker chick and the thought of carrying a frilly bouquet is just out of the question?

In a way, the answer is always the same: It's essential that the bouquet complement the outfit, the occasion, and most important, the bride.

Getting to know the brides-to-be who come to us is one of the most rewarding parts of our work. We often form lasting friendships as we visit the markets, develop the themes, and help decide the decor details. We ask a million questions in order to understand what the bride is really dreaming of: Is it a tiny nosegay beautifully tied to an heirloom Bible passed down from mother to daughter over the course of several generations? Or a wispy gathering of wildflowers loosely tied with a velvet ribbon that recalls memories of childhood summers? Is it a cascade of fragrant apple blossoms that transports her back to her grandparents' orchard, or is it that fantasy bouquet inspired by a beloved icon of the silver screen—Audrey Hepburn, perhaps?

We designed *To Have & To Hold* to be a friendly guide through this maze, to not only inspire but to liberate the bride so she can bring a truly personal style to her bouquet. It's an easy-to-use reference that explores the flowers available each season as well as those available year-round, the many varied styles and shapes that bouquets can take, and a variety of handle treatments that complete the flowers and add to their natural beauty. We've even included a "pricing meter," based on New York City retail prices (of course, the prices in your hometown will vary), to give you an idea of how much a bouquet might cost: $25–$100 (🌹), $100–$250 (🌹🌹), $250–$350 (🌹🌹🌹), $350–$500 (🌹🌹🌹🌹). It's a kind of *vade mecum*—a reference manual to "go with me." We can't physically take each of you on our personal market tour to help you choose colors, shapes, and patterns, but through this book we can be with you every step of the way.

FAR RIGHT: An increasingly popular stand-in for the traditional bridal bouquet, petite sprays of lilies of the valley adorn a small heirloom Bible, this one passed down through four generations of brides. 🌹🌹

The groom's boutonniere perfectly complements his bride's "bouquet." 🌹

Spring

Fresh, promising, new, and newly renewed, spring is invincible. Out of impossible winter, it defied all odds and plowed forward, love, hope, charity in tow. And now look at it, so indefatigably happy. Rain breaks into rainbows (corny but true), and not only in the sky: Those rains lead to mayflowers (no Pilgrim jokes, please), April flowers, March flowers . . . Who are we kidding? This season is nothing but glorious flowers and birds and bees and everything else Mr. Cole Porter lionized.

Okay, you're choosing from among the great, zealous, optimistic gardens of the season, so what do you go with? The pricey but splendid peony? Roses? Always nice. The anemone is seriously elegant, the daffodil ceaselessly sunny, the grape hyacinth a slice of a clear spring day. Pansies, hydrangeas, hellebores, tulips, fritillarias, lilies, sweet peas—if the list seems to go on forever, it's because it pretty nearly does.

This is the moment when not only plants burst forth but trees and bushes, too. Branches offer intoxicating possibilities—azaleas, dogwoods, the flowers of the apple tree, to name a few—with blooms and fragrances that you won't find any other time of the year.

So much to choose from—such a pleasant predicament.

LEFT: The chic white *Allium neopolitanum* is an esteemed member of the ornamental onion family.

CENTER: Coral charm peonies always provide a dense burst of color.

OPPOSITE: A sophisticated mix, perhaps for a wedding in a shaded forest glen: Eucharis lilies, also called Madonna lilies (the flowers that look a little like white daffodils with green centers), maidenhair fern, alliums, phlox, green hydrangeas, Bianca roses, and interwoven hosta leaves are caught with a gauzy length of white organdy ribbon.

Azure Glamour
Grape Hyacinths

Blue as a sparkling sapphire, a bouquet of grape hyacinths is like holding a piece of the spring day sky. With colors so intense they announce themselves from a distance, these puffy clusters exude a luxuriance matched only by their intoxicating scent.

Take the exquisite bouquet on pages 18 and 19: Hydrangeas, pansies, and even the curlicue staffs of the Uluhe fiddlehead fern serve as partners in glamour when matched with this flower's lush, sumptuous beauty.

The buds, ranging from cobalt to pale baby blue and clustered in bunches like grapes (and thus the name), offer an extraordinary sweep of possibilities that allow them to combine easily with flowers of similar hue or in striking contrast.

In this combination, a monochromatic mix of grape hyacinths amid sprinkles of tweedia are pleasantly set astir by the inclusion of pale, velvety roses. (Though roses are available year-round, tweedias and hyacinths are especially abundant in spring.)

Consider the basic elements of this composition. Note that this bouquet is

really a bundle of several smaller clusters of three, four, and five blossoms of various flowers. In short, a bouquet of mini-bouquets!

Note, too, that the contrasts here don't end with color. It's also about mixing flowers of different textures and sizes, where countless tiny petals act as a foil to the larger blooms.

Of course, as you mix, proceed with a touch of restraint. Going too far—garnishing with small dots of white baby's breath, for instance—would have transformed this charming confection into a busy mess.

Finished simply with a handle laced in overlapping lavender satin ribbons, this dense and heady formula makes for a visual feast able to take its place in the most formal of settings.

For all the power of its azure blue, however, the subtle side of grape hyacinth's colorful luster comes to the fore when used to punctuate a bouquet of fiercely purple pansies. Pansies, often mistakenly considered too fragile to withstand the rigors of a long day of wedding festivities, hold up exceedingly well in a bouquet. Just as you can make a statement by employing common materials in newfound ways, go beyond the rigid confines of how you normally think of flowers. In cases like this, expect gloriously uplifting results.

Grape hyacinths also promise a final plus: With these in hand, the bride always carries the requisite "something blue."

Like daffodils, grape hyacinths grow from bulbs, so in the seasons following their first planting, they continue to spread and become more and more plentiful with the passing years.

FOLLOWING PAGES: White majolica roses nestle among clusters of grape hyacinths and fine sprinkles of baby blue tweedias. 🌸🌸🌸

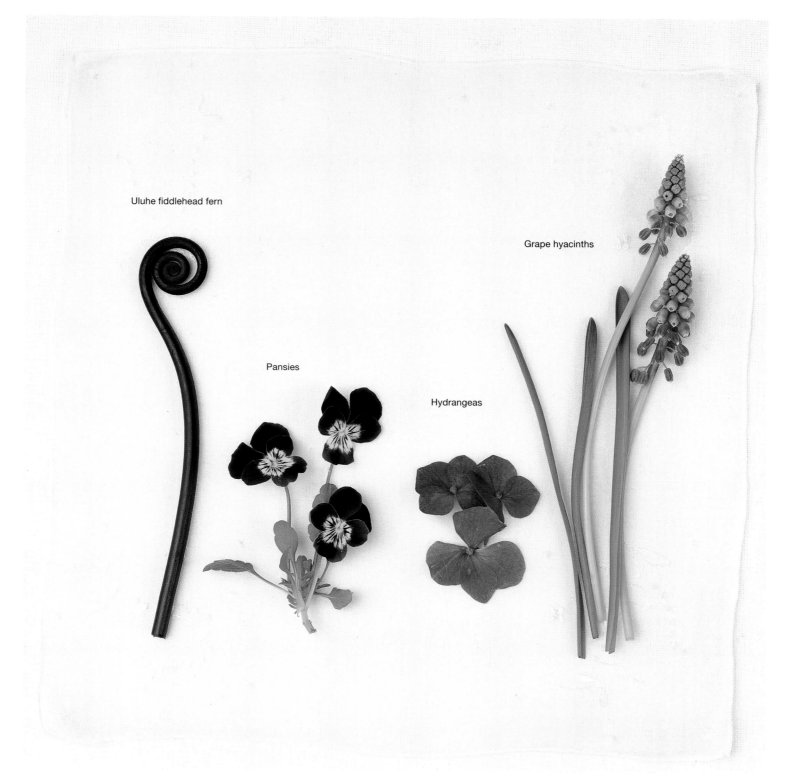

Uluhe fiddlehead fern

Pansies

Hydrangeas

Grape hyacinths

In this bouquet, the stem treatment goes luxe with a wrap that would border on prim if it weren't for the boldness of the violet ribbon contrasted with a single vertical panel of lavender fringed in purple. Pulling it all together is a short row of matching antique buttons from a collection of the bride's grandmother. Yes, it's meaningful, but it's a lot of fun, too. 🌼🌼🌼

Blooming Branches
Flowering Trees and Shrubs

Flowers flow from more than just bulbs and seeds. Look up: Overhead, trees often shade us with some of the world's most exquisite blossoms. Crab apple, dogwood, and cherry trees, along with bushes such as lilacs and azaleas, provide fragrant sources of delicate flowers that can be presented on their own or easily mixed with non-branch specimens to create uniquely enchanting bouquets.

With the proper selection and pruning, flowering branches provide an alternative that transforms gangly branches into pithy but lush floral wonders. The first step to "mastering the branch" is to realize all the possibilities. There are many varieties of lilacs, for example, with colors ranging from deep purples to chiffon whites; the lyrical blossom of the dogwood runs from milky white petals peppered with tiny splotches to gentle ivory hues streaked with burgundy. And branch flower stems aren't necessarily large or unmanageable; usually, they're no thicker than a daffodil's. Their sturdiness makes them good choices for canopies and chuppahs, easily interwoven with ivy and other blossoms.

Branch flowers mix well with other blossoms—the spare dogwood, for example, works best when it's filled out with flowers such as azaleas, heirloom garden roses, and sweet peas.

The one thing branch flowers aren't suited for is boutonnieres. The tiny woody branch of a single bloom usually doesn't hold sufficient moisture to get through a lengthy ceremony. Instead, select a flower of a similar color or one that complements the season.

To keep the flowers fresh, cut (at an angle, of course), then slice vertically up the stem about one inch. This helps the branch drink up enough water until it's time to go to work.

Handle with care: Unlike the sturdy crab apple, pink dogwood blossoms are relatively fragile and "crash" in high heat.

CLOCKWISE FROM TOP LEFT: An azalea branch; a rounded bouquet of crab apple 🌸🌸; a crab apple branch; a wax flower, crab apple, and white ribbon hair adornment.

OPPOSITE: A bouquet of azaleas, heirloom roses, and sweet peas, bound together with an heirloom handkerchief. 🌸🌸🌸

Sunshine Bouquet

Daffodils

Ten thousand saw I at a glance, Tossing their heads in sprightly dance."

When Wordsworth dreamily described a gently waving field of daffodils more than a century ago, he gave fitting homage to a delicate blossom whose very mention conjures the promise of spring.

With names such as Trumpet, Romance, and Lemon Glow, daffodils embody the delighted renewal of the season. Though they typically contain a single corona surrounded by a star of six petals, other breeds offer multiple layers of smooth, frilled, or fringed petals.

Some question yellow as a wedding color and, by extension, the use of daffodils. Let's put an end to that right now: Every color is beautiful, and each serves at the pleasure of the bride. That includes yellow, which represents gold, happiness, sun, and energy. On a day you want to radiate light, why not choose a flower that does just that? A cluster of daffodils is spring itself, a bouquet of sunlight.

And if yellow is absolutely not your choice—hey, it's your wedding—but daffodils are, don't worry: The flower ranges from snowy white petals with startling orange coronas—the "cup" at the center of the flower—to pale tangerine and even lime green.

One of the best things about daffodils in spring is that they are an amazing bargain. To be sure you have enough good blossoms on the day of the wedding, buy 100 and select the best 60 or 70 for the bouquet.

Some people interpret the low cost and easy glee of daffodils to mean an

Because the color yellow is so often associated with friendship, people sometimes avoid using it in a wedding. But there's no need to dwell under such a limiting shadow. These Tahiti narcissuses are yellow at its brightest and happiest, holding the promise of spring, energy, and warmth on the bride's sunniest day.

informal flower. It's true that a handful of these tied with a simple ribbon would be perfect for a low-key afternoon affair. But when wrapped in an overlapping matching ribbon or a stem treatment tied in an heirloom handkerchief, they take on a very dignified profile.

Blending with other flowers and handles extends your options. Mixing them with tulips, for example, formalizes the presentation. Wildflowers and daffodils wrapped in a cute row of flowered ribbon bows, on the other hand, are breezy and fun. A variety of daffodils mixed with euphoebias surrounded by hosta leaves, held with a simple slip of satin ribbon, is the very essence of chic.

Four days before the wedding, buy daffodils with a closed bud, with the hood of the bud starting to pull back. Stems need to be firm and a bold green; a rubbery, flexible, pale stem means an old flower.

As you should with every flower, give newly bought daffodils a fresh angle cut, place them in cool water, and put them in bright light but not direct heat. They'll open in about a day and a half. At that point, they can be recut and placed in cold water. This should put them on schedule to open fully in the next two and a half days in time for the wedding. Should they be slow to open, recut them and place them again in cool water.

Keep in mind that the stems exude a sap that turns vase water murky and is poisonous to other flowers, so change the water daily to avoid this problem.

Avalanche narcissuses (top left), surrounded by euphoebias, hosta leaves, and ferns, are bound together with an appropriately cheerful ribbon. 🌼🌼 A clutch of cream pencil tulips and geranium narcissuses (top right) are collared by a beaded embroidered hanky, a family heirloom brought from the old country by the bride's great-grandmother. 🌼🌼

FOLLOWING PAGES: The groom's boutonniere (left) draws its design from the bouquet's handle treatment and its showy Soleil d'Or narcissuses. 🌼🌼 A close-up of an Ice Follies daffodil (right) reveals a softly gathered, velvety corona.

The Essence of Chic

French Anemones

Delicate and sophisticated, the French anemone travels in very nice circles indeed. Its large black center, akin to a plush velvet button covered in countless ebony pushpins, lets you know that this is a flower that certainly knows how to play dress up.

Is your bridal color scheme black and white? Look no further. The dark center and surrounding buttercream petals work exquisitely well in the most formal of settings, and look stunning in black-and-white photographs.

For all its serious elegance, this is also a flower with immense versatility, making it equally at home where the atmosphere is more casual. It's so downright cute that it can switch from formal to casual in a wink. Whatever the case, you can proceed with confidence, because this flower carries such substantial beauty and elegance that it fits in, chameleonlike, in any situation.

And not just for the bride. If the bridesmaids are to be decked out in slender black cocktail dresses—and many brides are choosing this option as a way to free their friends from the terribly dated notion of a onetime-use chiffon number—expect the French anemone to be a stupendous addition. As for the groom and his groomsmen, few boutonnieres offer the cool, urbane look of this flower.

One note of caution: All that elegance, power, and versatility come at a price. This is one of the more expensive flowers in the floral palette, so prepare for a little sticker shock.

Because French anemones sprout from curvy, fragile stems that resist straightening with wires, a bouquet will have naturally occurring gaps. In this bouquet, we've filled those spaces with sweet peas, which complement and accentuate the lustrous, pale tones of the petals. To heighten the sense of elegance, we've trimmed the handle in a duet of black bows, making it a perfect match for formal wear.

Boldly Modern

Spring's Green Bouquets

Time was, the only color that never served as the main component of a bridal bouquet was green. It was relegated to the role of filler, an inexpensive background, always—dare we say it—a bridesmaid, never a bride. Not so long ago, a green bouquet was nothing short of taboo.

No more. Green is a color whose time has come, a powerful statement of utter modernity. Why do some of the most chic hotels in Florida's South Beach place a single green apple in each room? It's not for the nutrition: This is fashion pure and simple, a way to decorate with a burst of natural color. Green has become a power player—and bridal bouquets are no exception.

How did it happen? How did green flowers, once only associated with dyed carnations on Saint Patrick's Day, acquire the panache to move to the realm of weddings? It's partly the rise in environmental consciousness, of course, but the major reason is that many flowers—including tulips and roses—now come in variants of green (chartreuse is an especially important new color) or shades close to green, thus expanding the available selection of flowers.

VERDANT SELECTIONS: Green flowers and varieties available by season

Spring: Viburnums, ranunculus, hellebores, white anemones (can be considered green when not yet mature), parrot tulips (can be considered green when not yet mature), lady's mantles, euphoebias

Summer: Herb foliage; blueberries and their foliage; early thistle; soft blossoms of meadow grasses, such as foxtail, fountain grass, penstemmon, wheat, oats, zinnias, marigolds, and nicotianas; amaranths; cockscombs; sedums

Autumn: Zinnias, marigolds, nicotianas, cockscombs, amaranths, gladiolus, Andes chamomile, spider mums

Winter: Amaryllises, hellebores

Available most of the year: Hydrangeas; anthuriums; Green God calla lilies; lisianthus; Kyoto Green, Kermit, or Yoko Ono chrysanthemums; cymbidium orchids; dendrobium orchids, bupleurum or hypernicum berries; Jade, Limona, or Super Green roses; Prado or Bells of Ireland carnations

In this extremely sophisticated mix, you'll find ranunculus, lady's mantles, veronicas, and bupleurums, spiked with thin stems of greenish-white lilacs, but not one bit of green filler. The handle completes the formal air of this nosegay, where a wrap of white organdy ribbon secured with pearl pins echoes the wedding gown. 🌿🌿🌿

FOLLOWING PAGES: This sphere of green boldly features scattered poppy pods, the bulbs that form after the poppy flower has wilted away, and tiny hypernicum berries, also known as Saint-John's-wort, surrounded by ranunculus, bupleurums, euphoebias, and snowball blossoms. Broad, firm hosta leaves act as curtains swirling amid the verdant mix. 🌿🌿🌿

Spectacular Sight
Hellebores

"Something different."

Ask almost any bride what she's looking for in her wedding designs, and those two words will be part of the answer. Whether the setting is black tie or backyard, she wants the event to have its own unique stamp. For the bride who marries in early spring, hellebores may provide the answer. Their quirky color palette skips from buttery lemon fringed in green to lilac to creamy white to speckled purple. And because hellebores aren't widely produced commercially, your bouquet will be a far cry from the ordinary.

The hellebore lives something of a dual life. Though it's an extremely fancy flower—and thus tends toward the pricey side—it's also very hardy. Then again, what would you expect from a flower whose lineage can be traced to native plants that grow on the rugged, windswept cliffs of Sardinia and Corsica?

And it's not just hardy in terms of its physical endurance. This beauty can

An array of hellebores, from the fresh greens of spring to soft whites tattooed with burgundy stippling, are complemented by white French anemones with inky black centers, wine-colored tulips, and fritillarias (or checkerboard lilies). The long green blades of the fritillarias' foliage break the composition with jazzy sparks, while a sheath of tropical printed fabric, underscored by an elegant lacing of violet velvet ribbon and rhinestone studs, bridges the transition from blossom to stem seamlessly.

stand up to tulips, astrantias, hydrangeas, French anemones, and fritillarias—
and even manage to steal the show.

The power of hellebores is particularly evident when the flowers are paired
with French anemones—a clear case of a flower being influenced by the company
it keeps. In any other setting, it might be the silken smoothness of the anemones
that held center stage, yet here hellebores are the marquee performer.

For all their supple elegance, though, these flowers don't make for rigidly
classic bouquets in any sense of the word, so feel free to work their exotic
personality to suit your tastes. Wrap the stems in raffia and transform them into
a country bouquet. Encase the handle in a feather-patterned cloth, lace it in thin
satin ribbon, and finish it off with cut crystals, and you've created a bouquet
that exudes showy sophistication, ready for black tie and tails. We meant it: This
is a hardy flower that can't be overdone!

Hydrangea

Hellebore

Hellebore

Astrantia

Fritillaria

French anemone

Tulip

White French anemones are sparingly interspersed among the wine-colored blossoms; they serve as incidental accents, and the bouquet stays grounded in its deep hues.

Going Solo
The Single-Blossom "Bouquet"

In the beginning, every bouquet starts with exactly one flower. Sometimes that's also where it ends. Think about it: Why does a bouquet even have to be a bouquet? Why not just a single perfect blossom?

We were working with a bride who at first didn't want a bouquet at all. Our barely hidden looks of astonishment notwithstanding, we swallowed hard and nodded to show we understood. But inside we knew that she simply had to have one. To move our point forward, we gently asked, "Whatever you like, but what on earth will you do with your hands during the ceremony?"

This gave her pause and gave us the opening we needed to determine that in fact it wasn't a bouquet that she objected to, it was the idea of carrying a traditional, staid posy. The answer to her qualms came in the form of a solitary eye-popping poppy, so spectacular that it speaks for itself. Its five fire orange, black-dotted petals arching around a massive black stamen had the stature (as did the bride) and mystique (again, as did the bride) to make this work.

Don't let the words *nontraditional* and *natural* mislead you into thinking this is a choice for casual weddings only. Our bride's gown was very formal, in fact, and the single flower only emphasized its elegance.

More common, though no less formal, is the single rose. A long-stem white rose, for example, tied with a white satin ribbon becomes a slender floral scepter in the hands of the queen for a day.

One of our brides was getting married to a man who had made a habit of giving her a single rose every Friday when they were dating (our type of fellow). At the ceremony, after she walked down the aisle and stood beside him, he gave her one white rose tied in satin ribbon, which served as her bouquet. It's a good example of looking to your own history to create your own unique bouquet.

ON THEIR OWN
Perfect single stems,
available by season

Spring
Peony
Japanese peony

Summer and Fall
Dinner plate dahlia
Giant sunflower

Winter
Amaryllis

Year-round
Long-stemmed rose
Casa Blanca lily

Leaving the stem exposed and allowing its own leaves to serve as adornment underscores the natural appeal of this single exuberant poppy. A simple strand of ribbon serves notice that this is a very special flower in a very special role.

Miss Popularity

Peonies

Few flowers engage the passions like peonies, a flower whose popularity easily dwarfs the much more common rose. There are peony festivals, peony conventions, peony societies, and peony science and research institutes. China offers tours tailored specifically to catch these fragrant blossoms at the peak of the season, such as visits in April to Luoyang, the "city of peonies," which has cultivated the flower since the Sui Dynasty in the sixth century.

It's hardly a mystery why these dazzling, robust blooms should be so popular—and why eight out of ten women pick them as their favorite flower. Available in an enormous panoply of colors and varieties ranging from thick clusters of seemingly infinite layers of petals to open blossoms with frilly contrasting centers, their splendidness seems to know no bounds. Ironically, the Victorian language of flowers translated peonies as "bashfulness." This is a flower that is anything but shy; it's nearly bursting with star wattage.

We normally recommend that a bouquet never hide the bride's waist, but because peonies are so voluptuous, it doesn't seem fair to limit the size. Better to go large and carry the bouquet to one side, beauty-pageant style. Weddings are one of the times in a woman's life when she should feel free to bathe herself in flowers, and if ever there were a flower that you could immerse yourself in, it's the peony. Also keep in mind that peony stems are relatively thick, so balance your desire to go overboard on the voluptuous blossoms with the realities of the amassed weight that the bouquet will take on. The march down the wedding aisle should never be akin to a training session at the gym!

Peonies are spring flowers, but when it's fall and winter in the northern hemisphere, it's spring and summer in New Zealand, from where we get most of them. That Down Under connection translates into a spring season that is many

Moderation in all things, as they say—including moderation. This bride is carrying something close to a bucket of peonies, mixed with flowers of wild sweet pea vine, but the bouquet's beauty is so awesome that the scale works. 🌸🌸

The Little Frogs
Ranunculus

In Latin, *ranunculus* means "little frog," but that quirky tag belies the profound exquisiteness of this bloom, which boasts colors as varied as white, yellow-gold, bronze, orange, scarlet, and a green that's close to emerald. That yummy spectrum, along with a moderate price and a sturdiness that maintains its good looks through even the longest event, make ranunculus a justifiably popular bouquet choice. And like many flowers, they can assume whatever posture an arrangement and treatment demand, from casual to formal.

Truth be told, ranunculus begins life as a rather ugly bulb. But from that brown, wrinkled kernel springs a magnificent, versatile flower that dons a striking number of guises: The pale California ranunculus opens to reveal a *pas de trois* of white petals encircling a black ring that surrounds a white center; the deep red ranunculus, on the other hand, sports an eccentric, variegated center that looks like a parrot tulip.

Like tulips, ranunculus are reasonably priced, but off-season—after early summer—costs escalate according to declining availability. When you buy them, examine the stems—again, like tulips—to be sure they're firm and a rich green; a spongy, pallid stem is a red flag. Unlike tulips, however, avoid tight, unopened blossoms that may never open. Opt instead for half-open blooms. (A healthy cut tulip, on the other hand, rarely stays closed.)

As for the source of the "little frog" sobriquet, there are two theories. The first is a twist on the fairy tale frog that becomes a prince. In this version, after

CLOCKWISE FROM TOP LEFT: No flower has cornered the market on color, of course, but that hasn't stopped the ranunculus from trying. Its range is vast—from this clean and crisp California white ranunculus, which opens to the palest of green centers ringed by a fine halo of golden yellow, to the ultrafeminine pink, proof that the softer side of the palette is pure elegance. New hybrids such as the Green Success ranunculus and the Red Success ranunculus with their protruding centers, in contrast, are the avant-garde in extreme vivid color.

ABOVE LEFT: The Japanese Tango peony, with its oversize petals, is like a child's charming drawing of a flower.

OPPOSITE: In a very formal treatment, three long-stemmed Scarlet O'Hara peonies, also from Japan, are left unadorned save for a narrow matching ribbon pinned in place with a single showy rhinestone. 🌹🌹

the frog's transformation into a dreadfully handsome prince, he strolled the countryside serenading nymphs with his enchanting voice. Unfortunately, that was about all the love he could muster since, alas, the poor boy was too shy to bust a move. Unable to fess up to his feelings, he eventually pined away and was turned into the flower that bears his name. The second theory refers to the resemblance of wild ranunculus petals to a frog's foot.

Let's go with theory number one, shall we?

This plush bouquet of red ranunculus sprouting among maidenhead ferns is strictly reserved for romantics: Maid Marian walking down the aisle through Sherwood Forest.

Let It Snow

Leucojums

Leucojum is known informally as the summer snowflake, but that's something of a misnomer since it usually blooms from late winter into spring. Come the hot days of summer, it's no more likely to be found than a—well, snowflake.

Nomenclature aside—okay, not aside so quickly: The name comes from the Greek for "white violet." It's a beautiful specimen that can be transformed from a drooping bell in the wild—it's a native of North Africa and parts of Mediterranean Europe, where it has been cultivated since the 1500s—into a spectacular bouquet performer.

These little guys are related to snowdrops, which first bloom in the late winter, often piercing the snow. But snowdrops aren't available commercially as cut flowers, so if you want a bouquet that signals the arrival of spring, the leucojum is your man.

One of the hallmarks of this flower is its delicate, tiny gold stamens, which are sheathed within each blossom and therefore are less likely to stain gowns with their dusty pollen.

Like slender flashes of emerald energy, tendrils of bribie pine needles sparkle among a cluster of delicate white leucojum flutes, each petal dabbed with a drop of shimmering green and centered by a tassel of gold. It's a bouquet that has all the characteristics of a fun, casual nosegay, were it not for the perfectly symmetrical collar of deep green lamb's ears. That elegant hexagonal boundary—Elizabethan in its stance and clarity—tied into place with a broad swath of muted gold ribbon translates into an entirely formal offering.

FOLLOWING PAGES: A look at leucojum in its natural state underscores the dramatic transformation these drooping bells of blossoms make when summoned to duty.

Black Beauty

The Rich, Deep Hues of Spring

Spring is, to be sure, light and sun and brightness. But it also has its dark side—deep colors so dense they defy all our notions of the season.

A good case in point is the scabiosa. Imagine being utterly charming, very popular, and darkly beautiful, yet stuck with the sad sobriquet *scabiosa*. Such is the fate of this yummy flower, most widely available in its darkest incarnation, a deep burgundy. Found from Asia and Africa and throughout the Mediterranean coastal areas, scabiosas have been cultivated since medieval times, prized for their purported power to cure scabies (hence the less than lovely name). Their common name is pincushion flower, a reference to the many tiny stamens that poke their contrasting heads above the densely packed petals, making the bloom appear to be salted with speckles of light.

No less intriguing are the brown puffed blossoms of smoke trees. In late May to mid-June, depending on the region, these trees blossom and, from a distance, their finely spun wisps, ranging from green to deep burgundy, make the tree look as though it's engulfed in large, moody clouds of smoke.

Pink lilac

Oregano

Smoke tree

Scabiosa

Astrantias

There is a, well, a dark side to these colors. They just don't play all that well in dark settings—evening ceremonies, for example. And even if you marry in bright daylight, your photographs might suffer: Black-and-white film won't distinguish among burgundy, deep violet, or any other hue; to the camera you'll simply be carrying a clutch of dark, dark gray.

And think twice if you've got plans for an aisle of sprinkled petals if your photographs are going to be black and white. The bridal path dabbed in pink may end up looking more like a soot-spotted carpet that someone forgot to vacuum.

DARK AND LOVELY

Our favorite deeply hued flowers and foliage available by season. In combination with pastels or brights, these rich, dark blossoms, leaves, and berries can anchor a bouquet, adding sophistication and depth.

Spring: Plum leaves, smoke bush, burgundy ranunculus, plum tulips, plum hellebores, deep ruby Red Charm peonies

Summer: Brown sunflowers, brown/gold marigolds, bronzy echinacea seedpods, burgundy Voodoo dahlias, chocolate cosmos, burgundy scabiosas

Fall: Chrysanthemums, amaranths, pear leaves, privet berries, bush ivy berries, antique hydrangeas (matured)

Winter and year-round: Black Beauty roses, Black Magic roses, Black Baccara roses, burgundy Abrakadabra roses, burgundy Hocus Pocus roses, burgundy Simsalabim roses, eggplant calla lilies, chocolate anthuriums, antique red anthuriums

This tightly scripted bouquet could easily be categorized as Victorian—its collar is literally straitlaced—were it not for its color story, a pink and brown combination that's ultrachic and terribly fashion forward. Intermittent stabs of pink lilacs jazz the deep-colored flowers as well as leaves in similar tones. That richness comes alive in daylight, making this an ideal bouquet for an afternoon affair. ❧❧

Lucky Charms
Sweet Peas

Whoever wrote the maxim that you can never be too rich or too thin probably didn't have the sweet pea in mind, but the rule certainly applies. Dubbed "delicate pleasures" by the Victorians and praised by Keats ("Here are sweet peas, on tip-toe for a flight . . ."), these blossoms offer both intensely rich colors and ultra-skinny stems, to say nothing of a mesmerizing fragrance.

"Delicate" is something of a misnomer. While the pose of the sweet pea is genteel, it's a hardy specimen cultivated into more than a thousand varieties and derived from the same family of the climbing vines that produces peas. It can survive frosts, and if it snows, expect its shiny green head to pop through—how do you think the snow pea got its name?

The flower's colors start out at fairly basic, though comely, creamy white, but from there it's like jumping into a box of Lucky Charms: candy orange, peppermint pink, deep purple, ripples of lavender, navy blue.

Gather those colors carefully, however. Count us among the designers with strong opinions when it comes to mixing and matching colors. The purple sweet pea is wonderful, and the pink sweet pea is very nice, but you'll never find us putting them together. As far as we're concerned, pink and purple should get no closer than where you find them in the dictionary. And, if we may, one more color no-no in case you're thinking of pairing yellow and pale pink: Your bouquet should evoke joy and wonder but never a handful of bathroom tissue.

Non-vining varieties of sweet peas usually have two to three blossoms per each incredibly lean stem. The upside of that slender silhouette is that you can mass these flowers together by the dozens and still have room for more.

This bouquet features no fewer than 125 stems, yet the girth is about the same as half a dozen roses. Should the urge arise, in fact, we could pack in even more and still be left with a perfectly manageable handle, though any light entering the bouquet may have difficulty escaping. Here the ultraslim waist of the bouquet is dressed in a perfectly chic kick skirt of fringed café au lait trim; a smart bow of russet silk finishes the "outfit."

Simply Spring
Tulips

Tulips *are* spring. The tightly clustered buds that unfurl into brightly colored cups—each perched majestically atop a long, slender reed of a stem—trumpet to the world that the long slog of winter is over and, gloriously, the time for renewal, rebirth, and a fresh new season has arrived.

So potent is the life force of these flowers that they continue to grow after cutting. Tulip bouquets composed the day before a wedding, for example, may grow another half-inch overnight, so it's important to remember to allow for the new size in the design.

When you bring home a wrapped bundle of cut tulips, expose the ends, give them a fresh cut, and place them in water, but don't remove the paper. For the next five or six hours, the flowers will acclimate themselves to their new environment and respond to the constraints of the wrap, sort of like a bone setting in a cast. Left on their own in a vase without wrapping, they would soon droop as they seek the path of least resistance; tightly bundled, however, they will be trained to stand straight. Once the paper is removed, they'll maintain their upright pose. Give them at least two days to fully bloom, the stems arching and growing, the blossoms leaning toward the light, imperceptibly swiveling to the cadence of the day.

Just as spring is its own moment in time, tulips have theirs. Even though worldwide production makes them available year-round—during winter, we see the first fabulous specimens of the year, grown in hothouses, in the flower markets—a flower so associated with spring makes it a poor fit for the heat of summer. For one thing, a tulip grown in summer is usually smaller, less vibrant, and almost certainly weaker. The stems won't be as strong, the blossom not nearly so showy. Summer heat is tough on them, forcing them to open, invert, and lose their petals prematurely.

CLOCKWISE FROM TOP LEFT: That special collection of vintage buttons can finally be put to good use as the "icing on the cake" for a bouquet handle treatment. These snowy white varieties will soon be culled to do duty for a classic white bouquet. Accentuating the long, slim glamour of the French tulip stems, a tiny belt of satin ribbon is fastened by two elegant buttons from Grandma's attic. A French tulip sheath evokes both the romantic glamour of yore and the height of modern, minimalist chic. This sumptuous variety has satin textured blossoms that rival the finest silks, and stems that can stretch up to three feet.

Most important of all, however, is the fact that a tulip used out of season is nothing less than inappropriate. Think of flowers as fashion—and a bouquet will be among the most prominent fashion statements of your wedding—and you'll understand the relationship of the season to the flower. You can buy tulips in the middle of summer, sure, just like you can find wool sweaters in the dog days of August. But do you really want to wear either to a summer wedding? Tulips are right for spring because that is their time in the world.

A bunch of Angelique tulips, with striations from green to white, will be equally at home in a bouquet of either color. 🌷🌷

OPPOSITE: The Canova tulip, with its elegant ruffled petals of pink that fade to soft white, is the perfect dash of sweetness in a bouquet.

CLOCKWISE FROM TOP LEFT: The variegated red-and-white double blossoms of the Carnival tulip are accentuated by the heads of the black stamens. The luscious pink Louvre tulip would be quite at home in Paris's Luxembourg Gardens. The Renaldo, a rich, burgundy tulip variety, is a perfect reminder of the many deep, rich notes of the spring color palette. With the look of lilies, Golden Pete pencil-point tulips resemble golden stars.

OPPOSITE: A bouquet of lavishly fringed Canova tulips is punctuated by interwoven leaves of scented geranium. A tailored jacket of pink and green complements the flower color story, and an elegant belt of the same silk is fastened by a chic mother-of-pearl buckle.

The popular Carnival parrot tulip has outcroppings of frilly edged petals. In this example, its fiery red-and-yellow combination sets the tone for a handle treatment of yellow ribbon offset by stripes of vintage red trim. The ink black stamens offer a sophisticated punctuation that keeps the bouquet from being too candy sweet. 🌹🌹

Dainty Tidbit
Pansies

"And there is pansies, that's for thoughts."

When Shakespeare gave those words to Hamlet's Ophelia centuries ago, he captured for the ages the dreamy, wistful nature of a flower whose yellow, red, white, and countless shades of purple have made it a garden favorite wherever the evening air can hold a chill.

A common misconception is that pansies are fragile—thus its employ as a schoolyard taunt. Note to the bullies: Pansies are tough. This is possibly the most sturdy of all the perennials, a durability that comes in handy when summoned for a nosegay that must perform long hours as a focal point.

As hardy as the pansy is, however, it's undeniably a dainty tidbit, a flower so literally sweet that its petals are often candied and used as a dessert decoration. Even when bunched together by the dozen, it remains a small bouquet, perfect for the bride who wants something of substance, but isn't interested in making it into a big deal, a bon mot instead of a shout.

A MATTER OF SCALE

Size does matter. Pansies—and the graceful bouquets they build—are ideal for the larger or smaller bride. For larger women, smaller bouquets allow her to project grace. An oversized bouquet often has the opposite effect. Tiny brides, too, benefit from scaled-down bouquets, but because they complement her smaller cast. The last thing a smaller woman wants is a large cascade or sheath that catches everyone's attention, but at her expense.

Flowers are fashion. Vivacious and ebullient bouquets are made for brides of similar demeanor and carriage, while sophisticated gentlewomen should avoid anything that's too showy, large, or loud. What looks dazzling on one can be embarrassingly gaudy on the next.

ABOVE: Although unusual to see pansies as a cut flower, why not buy a couple of flats and harvest the blossoms yourself?

OPPOSITE: From ordinary to fabulous in a flash: The pansy readily turns into a surprising and wondrous bouquet.

The Good Book
Flowers and Psalms

The bride can carry more than a bouquet. An heirloom Bible—a gift from mother to daughter perhaps—is a note only sweetened by flowers.

The Bible, the ultimate symbol of Judeo-Christian faith, is an important religious statement. For deeply devout couples, holding one throughout the ceremony marks a commitment that draws strength well beyond the two who stand before the altar.

The book that's included in the bride's bouquet needn't be a religious text in the strictest sense of the word, but rather something that holds spiritual value for the couple. One bride we know carried a small sketchbook that her groom had filled with tiny drawings while the two were courting.

Either way, the look is modest, elegant, and gently pleasing to the eye.

White bleeding hearts share bookmark duties. 🌹

OPPOSITE: Delicate grape hyacinths float on a book of prayer (left). 🌹🌹 A wafer of a book (right) bears a single tiny stem of penstemon under a simple bow, a stunning contrast to the bride's embroidered gown. 🌹

Summer

"Summer idyll" says it all: the one season associated with poems and prose that captures the essence of simple, easy charm. Even the gods use it as playtime: According to tales dating back to the ancients, summer is universally loved—we dare you to find even one legend about any heavenly donnybrooks during June, July, or August.

Yes, there are mosquitoes and humidity—did we say brutal heat?—but while you keep those very real factors in mind, you might also be concentrating on the glory of the season: warm city nights on rooftops and days at the beach—heavenly, lazy days at the beach.

Dahlias, the peonies of summer, take center stage with colors as vivid as a sunset. And thanks to wide availability, they're quite affordable. Luxurious calla lilies offer glorious color from stem to bloom. And who can look at black-eyed Susans or sunflowers or daisies without feeling the season?

For weddings at the beach, shells look sweet in bridal bouquets. Tropical settings open the door for lush floral varieties—hibiscuses, orchids, pitcher plants. Red peppers and other peppy elements can be stirred in to make a summertime bouquet as hot as you like it.

The heat and sometimes tough environment that summer creates calls for sturdy yet sumptuous choices such as cosmos, zinnias, and marigolds. And then there is the rose. Wildly popular all year long, it has a field day, literally, in summer.

Take your pick, right from the garden.

The gangly elegance of the clematis (left), a flowering vine that usually finds a home climbing a garden wall, can be tamed into a beautiful cascade bouquet.

OPPOSITE: Pink majolica spray roses not only produce multiple blossoms on a single stem, but the blossoms are in a variety of stages of opening, from tight buds to full blooms.

Song of the Sea
Beach Bouquets

When designing your wedding, look to your surroundings. From full-blown formal parties at the Rainbow Room to Las Vegas ceremonies presided over by an Elvis impersonator, all weddings are in a sense "local." A garden wedding calls for a bouquet that looks as though it was picked from the garden itself; all the better if it was. And seaside weddings? Well . . . they just about beg to have sand and sea, shells and dune grasses, rambling roses, cattails, polished beach glass—anything found at the beach—incorporated in the decor, and most especially in the bridal bouquet. And why not mix ocean and flowers? Conch shells are found in gardens; gardens can come to the beach.

Gifts from the ocean: Gluing shells to 18-gauge straight wire (available from floral supply and craft stores) brings the sea to a bouquet made for a ceremony at the shore.

OPPOSITE: The last thing you want your bouquet to be is boring, and boring is about the last thing you'd call this nosegay of flowers, ornamental grasses, foliage, and shells. This maritime masterpiece is cinched by a wide, two-tone blue-and-white bow that secures the stems and adds a jaunty flare to the nautical theme. It's so cliché that it works! 🌺

Farm Fresh
Greenmarket Finds

The fresh provisions of a bustling farmer's market often include delights beyond gastronomy. We relish the opportunity to explore the local farmer's market near our studio in Brooklyn and check out the latest harvest from the gardens. Trucked in from small upstate New York farms by the growers themselves, these beauties are picked only hours before arriving in the city. You'd have to pick them yourself to get any fresher flowers.

If you decide to get your flowers from the farmer's market, visit it in the weeks or even months before your ceremony. Get to know the farmers and their flowers, and find out what will be in full bloom and available around the time of your wedding.

In order to add the peppers and rose hips to this bouquet, we created "stems" by piercing them with 18-gauge straight wire (available from floral supply and craft stores).

OPPOSITE: This fiery bouquet, teeming with verve and passion, was plucked from the buckets of a well-stocked farmer's market in New York City. Chocolate cosmos (they really smell like chocolate) are our starting point; a deep color offers an interesting contrast to the bright dahlias, zinnias, and heleniums of summer. The feathery spears of flaming celosia, or feather cockscomb, really set the bouquet afire; and the fresh hot peppers and rose hips turn this into a bold—not to mention unusual—arrangement, perfect for daytime or outdoor ceremonies. The bright, striped ribbon that holds it all together looks as though it was created for the bouquet, but it's really the bouquet that was created for the ribbon, which our bride and her fiancé found on a trip to Mexico.

Versatile Dazzler

Dahlias

Dahlias are the peonies of summer. Blooming from the hottest days of the season until the first frost of fall, these robust blossoms run the gamut from pale whites and pastel pinks and lavenders to blinding fuchsias and hot pinks. Some are only two inches wide, while others are as large as dinner plates—spectacular blooms that can be a full foot across. And these are strong flowers that can still look beautiful a week after cutting.Their diversity of shapes, from spiky, spare tendrils to those with more romantic, blousy layers of lavish petticoats, makes them a versatile bouquet choice.

This is an increasingly popular flower, thanks in part to their availability—they're not only grown throughout North America but are now also widely cultivated in Holland. (The Dutch imports, however, can barely compete with their cross-Atlantic cousins: American blossoms are much more showy.)

Another reason dahlias are being used more and more is that they can be a money-saving option: A large, dazzling bouquet of these beauties costs about the same as two or three stems of a pricey out-of-season flower.

Speaking of budgetary constraints—no show of hands necessary—always use those financial limitations to your advantage stylistically. Do what you can afford, but do it well. That way, whatever you choose to do, even if it's two or three exquisite flowers tied together with a crimped ribbon, it looks like a design decision, not a lack of funds.

Dahlias are dressed up with salvias and funnel-flowered pitcher plants that match the dahlias' rich pink, then neatly tied with vintage lace trim, vintage buttons, and a satin bow.

Dahlias come in an astonishing variety of colors, sizes, and petal shapes, but they all have a consistently sunny appeal. Ranging from two inches in diameter to an astonishing ten to twelve inches across (dinner plate dahlias), this flower can hold up remarkably well to the heat of summer.

OPPOSITE: Neon Splendor, Tony's Orange, and Smokey Gal dahlias provide a handful of orange, save for the tiny jolts of yellow buds (baby offshoots from the same stems). A filmy cascade of organdy ribbon softens the brightness with the right amount of romance. 🌹

Mixed with foxtail and coin grasses, chocolate
cosmos and astilbes, this cascading dahlia
bouquet is ready for a ceremony that's more of a
country affair; one can easily imagine the bride
arriving sidesaddle on a pony, the sheath of
flowers cradled in her arm. The dramatic trail of
wide, striped grosgrain is sporty and graphic,
mirroring the extreme contrast of the flowers—
deep, rich darks with flashes of bright white.

Regal Bearing
The Biedermeier Bouquet

Following the French Revolution, Europe's remaining monarchs instituted strict societal reforms intended to avoid the disaster that had befallen King Louis XIV and Marie Antoinette. In the Alpine region, that meant shutting down any organization, club, or meeting room that might foster revolt. Instead, family ties were cultivated, in emulation of the royal family of Vienna. The Biedermeier period began—mannered, reserved, royal, and structured. (The term *Biedermeier,* once considered derogatory, comes from Gottlieb Biedermeier, a pseudonym collectively used by several German writers whose articles sought to puncture the style of the day, albeit behind the safety of a fake name.)

The bouquet style of the era bears the same name and the same qualities. Set in concentric circles around a single blossom, the Biedermeier radiates out with rows of contrasting elements. This is among the most structured of bouquets, yet its confinement, control, and stylizing give it a regal elegance.

This is not the bouquet for a barefoot country lass who plans to get married down by the river. This is meant for the bride who relishes structure in her life and appreciates things being done just so. Ironically, she's also likely to be thoroughly modern. At a time when minimalism in architecture and style is prized, the formality of the Biedermeier feels very contemporary. And though the Biedermeier is rooted in the nineteenth century and makes an undeniable historical reference, the sheer fact that it's not often seen gives it a freshness.

To create a Biedermeier, begin with a favorite flower for the center, then choose flowers in a complementary palette and use them to paint the form. Here, our form is a radiant circle. We started with a single pink chrysanthemum surrounded by loops of ribbon. We added more chrysanthemums, then celosias, then rows of yellow-green and pink chrysanthemums, and, finally, sprigs of solidaster.

Chive

Veronica

Scabiosa

Ageratum

Dusty miller

FOCAL POINTS
Perfect Biedermeier centers

Rose

Stephanotis

Clustered lily of the valley

A small peony

Hyacinth

Clustered grape hyacinth

Narcissus

Cabbage

Dahlia

Zinnia

Carnation

RUNNING IN CIRCLES
Flowers for concentric Biedermeier rings

Calla lilies

Sweet peas

Cymbidium orchids

Spray roses

Carnations, mini-carnations

Wax flowers

Baby's breath

Craspedias

Chamomile blossoms

Chive blossoms

Hydrangeas

Solidagos (goldenrods)

Eucalyptus berries

Hypernicum berries

Privet berries

Ferns

Galax leaves

Cedar or juniper boughs/sprigs

Chrysanthemums

This Biedermeier's building blocks include matching ribbon (three hues of satin chosen to complement the variety of floral hues in the bouquet), which will be fashioned into a formal wrap for the stems. A dramatic scabiosa specimen serves as the starting point—and focal point—for this bouquet of sophisticated plums, lavenders, purples, and contrasting dusky grays. Around it we placed tiny plum alliums, pale dusty miller, and a collar of lavender ageratums. The drama comes from a flourish of gooseneck Veronicas that resemble miniature purple parasols tightly closed up and, as a quiet finishing touch, yet another round of dusty miller.

From the Heavens

Cosmos

Among horticulturists, cosmos are what's known as a "tough love" plant. When given too much care, they tend to get spindly and stingy with their blossoms. Subjected to brutal heat, low soil fertility, and drought conditions, however, and the plant gushes forth with multiple, glorious blooms.

This ability to make the most of the worst soil conditions has made cosmos an extremely popular garden variety. The flower ranges from close-to-the-ground specimens to varieties that can stretch up to four feet tall.

Spanish missionaries first discovered the symmetrical delights of these flowers in Mexico. They named them cosmos, a word derived from the Greek word for a universe that is ordered and harmonious, a reference to the flower's simple arrangement of evenly spaced petals.

SOME LIKE IT HOT
Heat-tolerant varieties

Calla lilies, cymbidium orchids, roses, sunflowers, black-eyed Susans, marigolds, zinnias, daisies, dahlias, PG hydrangeas (when mature in September/October, they become tinged with pink), wax flowers, cockscombs, chrysanthemums, thistles, carnations, baby's breath, limoniums, strawflowers

This clustered country bouquet of contrasting hues—from crisp summer whites to hot, deep fuchsias—represents the spectrum of colors from the cosmos garden. An elegant French braid on the handle transports this creation from the roadside farmstand to the wedding aisle; an extra-long pair of ribbon tails dropping beneath the bow form two tiny veils gently grazing the outside of the bride's hands.

BOUQUET HANDLES

Just as a bouquet is an accessory for the bride, the handle is an accessory for the bouquet. Handles are things of beauty in their own right. They also serve important functions: protecting the hands from thorns, keeping white gloves white, and holding together what may be a disparate set of stems and wires of varying thickness and sturdiness, allowing the bride a comfortable grasp.

Handles also know how to play dress up and provide an additional opportunity to make a personal statement. With imagination and inspiration from unusual places, you can create an expression that is at once unique and beautiful—an heirloom handkerchief, a swatch or buttons from your mother's gown, batik from a trip to Thailand, an old bookmark—anything treasured. Think belts and buckles or shoelaces Use a zipper. Consider macramé. This is your chance to enhance your bouquet with history, tradition, fashion, and personality.

Ribbons are popular, in part because they always fit: Regardless of the content or size of the bouquet, a ribbon will always be able to wrap and hold the stems. Try pinning it in place with jeweled studs or a row of antique buttons.

With some stems, it's easy to wind up with a handle the size of a beer can. In cases like that, cut off the stems and replace them with wire inserted in the head of the flowers; this will bring the handle down to an ideal width of about two inches. Still, it's usually good to have a bit of the stems peeking out; the handle is a way to encase the stems, not hide them.

Finally, perhaps now is as good a time as any to say a special word about the white plastic cones that some national floral chains think are appropriate as handles, and that special word is *never*. Or more to the point, *never*. The cones—really poor cousins of the elegant silver tussie mussies popular during the Victorian era and that have lately staged a mini-comeback—are usually stuffed with a bit of green oasis which, in turn, is stuffed with flowers like an oversized scoop of ice cream. Sorry, but we just don't think they're worthy of you.

This handsome handle treatment is relatively inexpensive and easy to achieve. A tightly woven French braid—no gaps—pulls the cosmos stems together. Each twist and turn of the ribbon is held in place with a pearl head pin, creating a row of buttons along the handle that echoes the string of buttons along the back of the bride's gown. The weave formalizes the bouquet and at the same time protects the bride's white gloves.

Begin about one-third of the way above the ends of the stems, which have been trimmed precisely to an even length. Wrap the stems, keeping the ribbon at its full width. To make the knots, simply crisscross the two ends of the ribbon, then reverse direction as the ribbon goes back around the stems, creating a seam along one side of the handle. Smooth the ribbon on the opposite side of the handle to create a flat, seamless surface. As each knot is placed cheek by jowl next to the other, the ribbon will get tighter, creating an elegant enclosure that prevents any peeking at the stems. As you tie each knot, pierce it with a pearl head pin; be sure the pin is inserted at an angle so the sharp end goes deep into the stems and doesn't come out the other side.

Herbal Delights
The Edible Bouquet

Oregano? Basil? Blueberries? In a wedding bouquet?

What might be considered outlandish when considered on its own can make perfect sense in the right context. A couple who run a gourmet food business asked us to design their wedding celebration. Because food is such an important element of their lives together, they wanted the event, right down to the bouquet, to reflect that fact.

The wedding was to be at a vineyard on Long Island's East End on a summer Sunday afternoon (the ever important location and context), and the bride was a most confident young woman, which is what allowed us to think outside the usual bouquet. We set out to examine the culinary possibilities, including spices and berries.

Still, for all the easy charm of time and place, the couple didn't want to give short shrift to elegance, so we devised a handle that reflected all the elements in the bouquet and that could only be called "rustic chic."

The result of this collaboration is on page 100. It may be true that you can't take the country out of the girl, but then again, who wants to?

DELICIOUS
Edible floral delicacies

Alliums

Calendulas

Carnations

Chrysanthemums

Citrus blossoms

Day lilies

Fennel

Gardenias

Geraniums

Herb flowers (chamomile, mint, basil, dill, rosemary, chive blossoms)

Jasmine

Lavender

Lemon verbena

Lilacs

Nasturtiums

Pansies

Queen Anne's lace

Roses

Scented geraniums

Violets

Smoke bush

Chive

Lavender

Foxtails

Blueberries

Sage

Scabiosa pod

Spirea

Ornamental oregano

Greek oregano

Lamb's ear

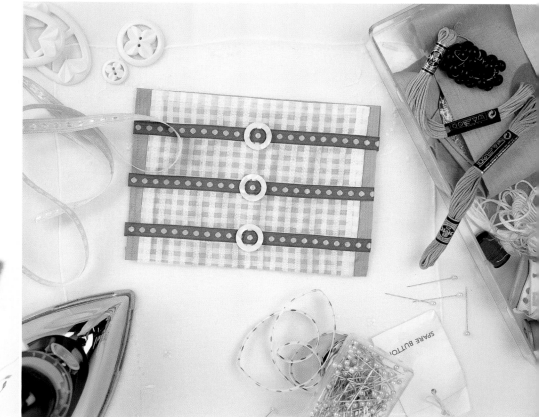

Moments before the bouquet is dressed, a tailored rectangle of silk is sized to wrap our handle perfectly. Narrow belts of dotted green are made from lengths of ribbon sewn to the jacket and held in place with mother-of-pearl buckles. One of a kind and utterly charming, the handle is just as integral to the look of the bouquet as the flowers themselves.

LEFT: This showy burst of summer disguised as a bouquet sports a country look, thanks to a plaid handle that wraps around grasses, herbs, and blueberries.

The Royal Standard
Roses

The "first o' flow'rs," said Robert Burns of the rose, and was he ever right. The sweep of color, the grace, the history: Roses are so well understood and broadly worshipped that they defy hyperbole. They swim in metaphor (bed of roses, mighty like a rose, rose-colored glasses), signify unbridled devotion (England's rose), and for centuries have engendered the adulation of the world's poets, artists, and lovers.

Cleopatra carpeted her palace floors with rose petals and used them to stuff her pillows. Sultans in ancient Baghdad perfumed their harem rooms with thousands of vases of rose water. Lovers forbidden to express their feelings openly in the harems used roses to secretly communicate—an open red rose proclaiming love and desire, for example, a yellow rose wondering if love was still there—which became the precursor to the Victorian language of flowers. When defeated Crusaders returned to Europe from the Middle East, they brought back roses, which were cultivated by monks as medicine long before rose hips were discovered to pack a wallop of vitamin C.

The unparalleled popularity of roses has sometimes worked against them, though, especially among more creative brides, who associate them with national florist chains and the cliché of baby's breath. Truly creative types, however, know better. The flower's incredible color palette, everything except blue and true black, though the ultra-dark reds get close enough to fool the eye; the variety of shape and size, from garden specimens to hybrids; and the year-round availability make roses worthy of consideration by even those who seek something really different.

Rosette-shaped garden roses are evocatively called Gina Lollobrigida—could a flower have a more sumptuous name? An embroidered handkerchief wrapped around the handle completes the yellow rose story.

Garden roses work just as well as long-stemmed varieties for bouquets, since they'll be cut anyway. (They smell like perfume, too!) In fact, rose stems are often replaced with wire to reduce the heft of the handle.

When you're buying roses, choose tight flowers, but not so tight they resemble bullets. There should be some indication that they're starting to open. (These days there's little difference between the fine smaller-headed specimens from France and Holland and the grander large blossoms from South America; both are reliable and open beautifully.)

When roses go bad, they rot from the outside. That's why you'll see people plucking bad petals before offering them for sale. Save yourself the heartache—those kinds will never open.

This brilliant panoply of pinks includes Soutine roses, rambling roses, and pink garden tea roses tied with an antique handkerchief. 🌹🌹🌹

OPPOSITE: Iceberg roses, as they appear on a single stem, offer multiple blossoms at their various stages of development, from buds to fully opened beauties.

The Good Onion

Alliums and Evening Primroses

TREATING STAINS

Always hold your bouquet just
a bit in front of you to avoid
staining your dress. If the
unthinkable happens, however,
try the following:

If the stain is small or easily
hidden in the folds of your
gown, just leave it alone. If it's a
sizable stain that just has to go,
dab it with cool water or club
soda on a white absorbent
cloth; place another white cloth
underneath to absorb both the
water and the stain. Never rub—
this will only force the stain
deeper into the fabric. (Don't try
this on silk or rayon—even if you
remove the stain, you'll wind up
with a permanent watermark; be
patient and wait until you can
have it dry-cleaned.)

For an emergency cover-up, try
talcum powder, cornstarch, or
another white powder.

Have the dress cleaned
professionally within a few weeks
of the wedding; be sure to point
out any significant stains.

During one of his many hissy fits aimed at grand literary dame Gertrude Stein, Ernest Hemingway attempted a taunt by twisting her famous line "A rose is a rose is a rose" into "A rose is a rose is an onion."

Too clever by half, Papa. Turns out the onion—or at least its flower—can be every bit as glorious and gorgeous as any rose.

Onions and herbs such as garlic often produce disarmingly sweet flowers (which often, the sensitive nose will note, carry the scent of their namesake savories). Using these beauties in wedding bouquets has a long history, dating back to when brides in ancient Rome and Scandinavia carried herbs to bring luck. For the modern bride, this type of selection is yet one more way to create her own personal statement.

Among the prettiest of this "luck-bringing" species, the allium is a flowering bulb that happens to be an onion. Its jaunty pose—tiny balls of multiple flowers—and colors of white, yellow, red, and violet makes it a natural for a delicate bouquet.

Gertrude (and, no doubt, Alice B. Toklas) would be proud.

This riot of yellow alliums and evening primroses is kept snugly under control with a short wrap of yellow-edged ribbon, saucily buttoned up with a row of yellow capped pins angled so as not to pierce through to the other side. In a nod to the natural beauty of the flowers, one or two inches of the stems escape from below the ribbon. And why not? Stems can be beautiful in their own right. 🌹🌹

Daisy Chain
Establishing a Theme

How many daisies have been sacrificed for questions of romance ("she loves me, she loves me not, she loves me . . .") is unclear, but they certainly are well suited for the duty. Spectacularly happy, indefatigably sunny, daisies radiate innocence and country charm. Yet with the right treatment, they can be transformed into an ultrasophisticated role.

The daisies on these pages also serve as a good example of how one single flower can advance an entire design theme. We all know that weddings can sometimes be overwhelming for a couple as they attempt to sort through so many choices and arrive at so many decisions. For them, the bridal bouquet can provide the starting point for the day's decorative motif and settle a host of design questions. Best of all, daisies are reasonably priced, so buy as many as you want to use to dazzling effect. Please do eat the daisies.

The daisy theme is appropriately extended to this flower girl's basket. Instead of tossing rose petals, an aisle of scattered daisy heads will beautifully lead the wedding party to the altar with a sweet, summery smile.

OPPOSITE: Though it might be a bit much to expect this combination at a formal evening affair, dressed with ferns, ivy, and white hydrangeas, this bouquet easily holds its own against the beautiful brocade and beading of the bride's gown. The larger daisy plays well against the tiny chamomile (yes, just like the tea), which echo the look of daisies, only in miniature.

CLOCKWISE FROM TOP LEFT: At the table, daisies make a smashing centerpiece; caught in a yellow ribbon, they also add to a napkin treatment beneath place cards. Bridesmaids' bouquets similarly draw upon the flower as its main feature, including a spine of sweet buttons in daisy caricature. 🌼 Daisies are the tassels on the pillow the ring bearer will carry down the aisle. The flower theme is carried through to a spectacular yellow-and-white cake trimmed with sweet blossoms along a ribbon of frosting at its base.

OPPOSITE: The groom and his crew each sport a single super-simple daisy boutonniere on their lapels. 🌼

Taking Center Stage
Black-eyed Susans

From the moment the season begins heating up, black-eyed Susans brighten the world with their perky yellow petals and dark brown/purple centers. And they're kind enough to stick around until October.

European settlers found this native American plant in abundance east of the Rockies. Black-eyed Susans are pretty impressive: They grow up to four feet tall and feature blossoms from two to three inches in diameter. They're also pretty pushy: Left to their own devices, they'll squeeze out other less aggressive plants. They're also among the most common of field flowers because they can grow in almost any soil.

Thanks to their sturdiness, these rugged beauties are among the first plants to appear after a forest fire. That hardiness makes them ideal for a summer bouquet, where they refuse to wilt even on the hottest day.

This summer bouquet was picked right from the garden. A long, narrow ribbon studded with gold flecks ties together black-eyed Susans, zinnias, green marigolds, Andes chamomile, a bit of pink hydrangeas, and Macarena spray roses the color of orange sherbet.

The Common Thread

Bridesmaids' Bouquets

Just as the dresses and accessories of bridesmaids should in some way relate to the bride's apparel, so should the flowers underscore that connection. One way is to build bridesmaids' bouquets from just one of the bride's bouquet flowers—just hydrangeas or just calla lilies or just roses; or perhaps each bridesmaid carries a different floral component of the bride's bouquet.

Another way is with color. If the bride is carrying yellow, red, orange, and green, for example, each bridesmaid can carry flowers that draw upon one single color from that story—one bridesmaid holding all yellow, another with all red, and so on. Of course, scaled-down versions of the bride's bouquet are beautiful for each bridesmaid as well.

No matter what path is taken, no one should ever carry a bouquet as large or as beautiful as the bride's. It's her day. She's the star.

This summer version of a mixed white bridal bouquet is no less opulent than its spring counterpart. Here dahlias, calla lilies, phlox, hydrangeas, and lisianthus—the flower that looks like a rose—produce a compact yet showy range of whites and off whites. 🌸🌸

FOLLOWING PAGES: The flowers of this same bride's bouquet are parsed into four pure specimen bouquets for her bridesmaids—a lovely sentiment that says, "You're part of me." (Clockwise from top) Lisianthus, white hydrangeas, phlox, and calla lilies are elegantly unified by both their monochrome hue and their coordinating handle treatment. 🌸🌸 Like buttons on the back of a gown, a fine spine of pearl head pins holds the French-braided satin ribbon in place and gives the flowers a wonderful air of formality. 🌸🌸

BLANCS DE BLANCS .

The white bouquet all year-round

Winter: Amaryllises, tulips, alliums, hydrangeas, anemones, narcissuses, snowflakes

Spring: Tulips, alliums, anemones, white grape hyacinths, narcissuses, daffodils, lilac, crab apple, Japanese quince, dogwood, jasmine, Eucharis lilies, peonies, ranunculus, garden roses, clematis

Summer: Daisies, chamomile, dahlias, Casa Blanca lilies, hydrangeas, phlox, Queen Anne's lace, lysimachias, Veronicas, roses, chrysanthemums, calla lilies, anthuriums, cosmos, hybrid delphiniums

Fall: Dahlias, hydrangeas, lisianthus, roses, orchids, snowberries, chrysanthemums, deco mums

Year-round: Carnations, freesias, baby's breath

Delicate, very special white perennials: Hellebores, lilies of the valley, columbine, bleeding hearts

Floral Décolletage
French Braiding

Some stems are gangly, others threaten with thorns, while others resemble stringy noodles al dente. Yet there are others—French tulips or even the amaryllis—that sport stems long and sleek, as elegant as the blossom they host. And sometimes those stems are an integral part of the blossom. Such is the case with the Hot Chocolate calla lily, where the rich burgundy of the flower seeps dreamily down the stems like a drip of Tiffany stained glass.

An open French braid makes the most of this beautiful situation. By sinuously slinking up and around the stems—while leaving significant portions of the stems exposed—this braiding technique offers the best of two worlds: The flowers are ensconced in a brilliant, elegant wrap, yet the stems are framed in diamond-shaped windows, each edged in satin.

French braiding is really simple: Begin with a nonwired ribbon of a color that complements the flower and is about the same width as a single stem. Lace from the bottom up, leaving a substantial portion of the stems unadorned below the ribbon line. Crisscross, leaving even intervals of bare stem, finishing up a few inches below the blossoms with a simple overhand bow.

OPPOSITE: Our bride's dress is perfectly in tune with the sleek silhouette of her bouquet.

Brown-Eyed Girl
Sunflowers

If you subscribe to fashion's new vocabulary—brown is the new white—then sunflowers, with their large brown centers must be the height of chic in the world of bouquets. But color *du jour* aside, sunflowers were cultural icons long before they were bridal bouquet favorites. Native Americans were dependent upon them (from sunflowers they made flour for bread and oil for cooking) and artists immortalized them (think of Van Gogh). Today, whole economies thrive on them (the Great Plains states have turned sunflower oil production into a mainstay of the region). And they're absolutely stunning; why else would so many tourists the world over make pilgrimages to Tuscany and the south of France for the simple pleasure of standing witness to radiant fields of sunflowers stretching for miles and miles?

Why not lasso that view for your wedding? Sunflowers equal summer, and they come in enough varieties to fit every kind of wedding, from casual backyard ceremony to big-city black-tie affair: Picture the classic sun-shaped field flower, or the pale Italian whites, or even the deep browns and sunset ambers of Evening Suns. As an added bonus, they're all extremely affordable and heat tolerant.

The cool bride who asked for this bouquet carried it at her outdoor afternoon wedding. The large brown centers of Claret sunflowers, edged with tawny orange petals, are complemented by striped pinwheels—French marigolds—in similar hues. The handle of the bouquet, outfitted in the alternating colored silk (again, playing off the burnt oranges and yellows of the blossoms) is held together by three tiny burnt-orange bows.

OPPOSITE: The sunflowers in this bouquet are smaller than the classic variety, have lemon yellow petals but the same large brown center. Here privet and hypernicum berries and sprigs of cedar dance around a sprinkling of yellow ornamental peppers. (A lot of people use fruit along with flowers in their bouquets; we say, why not open it up to vegetables as well!)

Painter's Palette
Summer's Color Wheel

A handful of summer: That's how a gorgeous interplay of colors reads when they're gathered together in a bouquet that bursts with all the hues and nuances of the season.

It's a deceptively simple mix. At first glance, bold color-mix bouquets appear to have been whipped up in an instant, but these are carefully studied arrangements, not unlike those that Matisse created in his wondrous oil paintings. His works display a charming insouciance, as though colors simply dripped on the canvas, then suddenly . . . another masterpiece! In reality, his paintings were deeply detailed in plan and construction, a labor made all the more difficult by the drive to disguise them as casual efforts.

In the world of flowers, the success of this kind of bouquet comes from mixing opposites on the color wheel—purples placed next to yellows, for instance, or oranges mixed with blues. This jars the senses into noticing not only each color but how each color reacts with its complementary color.

If someone thinks it all just fell together in an instant, take it as the ultimate compliment.

Purple spurts of ageratum, salvia, and penstemmon play against yellow Andes chamomile and speckles of hypernicum—aka Saint-John's-wort—berries. Its casual "just randomly been plucked from the garden" message is telegraphed by various colors, textures, and shapes.

True Blue

Delphiniums

Delphiniums have long been a favorite flower of gardeners, but they rarely appear in traditional bridal bouquets since their pure blue color is more often associated with masculinity. A pity: Their long, densely flowered stems can make them ideal for over-the-arm sheaths, and their stunning blue is neither male nor female, but just plain breathtaking.

The stems grow up to three and a half feet long, two-thirds of which bear its long flowers (which also come in white with tiny black centers). Pull together several stems of various lengths for a natural fall that gushes with color and makes a truly royal statement.

Delphiniums are their showiest in early summer. Like many flowers, including poinsettias, parts of them are toxic, so handle them carefully—and be sure Fido doesn't end up chomping on the bouquet!

BEST BLUES

Spring sets the bar, but summer is prime time

Spring

Grape hyacinths

Hyacinths

Summer

Bella donna delphiniums

Hybrid Dutch delphiniums

Tweedias

Bachelor buttons (cornflowers)

Hydrangeas macrophylla

Sea holly (thistle)

Grape hyacinths

Hyacinths

This hybrid delphinium arm sheath runs the gamut from pale lavender to deep royal blue—perhaps your "something blue"?—to saturated purple. It naturally drapes beautifully over the arm, and a fine trail of satin gilds the lily. 🌹🌹

Christmas in July
Red-and-Green Bouquet

It's easy to put the mark of summer on a bouquet, even when it features a mix of red and green, a color combination so associated with Christmas that it's hard to imagine it except in December.

A good start is subtlety, avoiding jarring color clashes and looking instead to softer greens that work with the reds. Tossing yellow into the mix—a look that comes across as natural because the colors are found in nature—gives the bouquet an even surer footing.

Leaves of the coleus, a common garden border plant, can provide a parallel variegation of yellow and red in a single leaf. They're fragile, so treat them gently: Keep them from extreme heat and handle them carefully, and they'll add a slice of vivaciousness.

This sprightly bouquet has summer written all over it, a point made all the more obvious by the gingham bow on its handle. Note, too, the variegated Papagallo roses. Their placement among chartreuse zinnias and deep pink hydrangeas makes their two-toned look blend perfectly with the other flowers. (Setting them among white flowers would have drawn too much attention to what many consider a second-tier flower.)

Autumn

As the year approaches the end of its life cycle, fall does the sensible thing: Jump off a cliff and go out in a blaze of color. The season isn't about foliage that's demure, precious, or shy; this is color without apology. No shade is too hot, no combination too bright. Yellow mums, blazing orange calla lilies, fire-red leaves: Fall has plenty of ways to integrate the warmth of the season.

While we love all the classic colors of fall, the season also offers a palette of soft whites and gentle yellows, chartreuses and purples equally deserving of our affection. Fashion-forward combinations such as brown and blue or brown and pink look fabulous this time of year. Even just a touch of brown makes any bouquet so season appropriate.

Harvest, bounty, cornucopia—it's all good enough to eat! Spearmint becomes a refreshing touch; ornamental cabbages center opulent Biedermeier bouquets; tiny apples grace a mix of hydrangeas and roses. Honey-scented andromeda, a spring flower from Australia that makes it a fall specialty here, comes into play.

So much goodness. No wonder people give thanks this time of year.

Buckets of sunset-hued chrysanthemums capture fall in all its burnt glory.

OPPOSITE: This yummy pink-and-brown number combines the palest whiff of pink majolica roses, Sahara roses, wax flowers, and rich brown photinia leaves, not as filler but as feature. A jacket of brown silk is trimmed with tiny mahogany buttons capped with a wide bow of pink silk taffeta.

A Walk in the Woods

Fall's Other Color Story

Creating a proper look for fall has its challenges. Sometimes our clients reject roses or other flowers strongly associated with spring, summer, or winter; they're looking for "something seasonal." But no one wants to carry a mini–harvest table. Even if the wedding is on Thanksgiving Day, we don't want to send a bride down the aisle clutching a cornucopia.

The solution is to skip typical fall colors—oranges, reds, yellows—and rely on other emblems (and colors) of the season, such as acorns, cedar, or even fruit in deep browns, greens, and grays. Think of taking a walk in the woods on a cool fall day. What do you see? Deep green mosses, a floor of brown leaves, nuts, and berries. Begin by gathering that color story into a bouquet, then add the very elements of the season itself, including wisps of cedar and jaunty capped acorns. Take that inspiration to the flower or farmer's market and you'll find an array of unusually hued blossoms to expand on this theme. Sunflowers, for instance, are available in many more varieties than the golden, iconic classic of Van Gogh's paintings. The rich, deep chocolate browns of the Teddy Bear sunflower and the chocolate cosmos (which actually emits the fragrance of chocolate) add a punctuation of dark beauty that is at once autumn personified and sumptuously unique.

GIFTS FROM THE BRANCH

Fall

Lady apples

Large crab apples

Ornamental pears

Champagne grapes

Acorns

Gourds and miniature pumpkins

Chile peppers on stems

Small artichokes

Small pomegranates

Winter

Key limes

Kumquats

Chestnuts

Unshelled hazelnuts, almonds,
   walnuts, Brazil nuts

Pine, hemlock, redwood cones

Feathers

Spring/Summer

Berries on their stems, such as
   blueberries or blackberries

Birds' nests

A sophisticated autumnal mix celebrates the season with a refreshing color palette. The chocolate browns that sinuously streak through the chartreuse coleus leaves are repeated throughout the bouquet. Chocolate cosmos, Velvet Queen sunflowers, cedar sprigs, lady's mantles, begonia leaves, and decorative acorns share the stage. A silk grosgrain ribbon of variegated greens and ivories lends an air of formality to these rustic forest finds.

Inspired Choices
Single-Flower Starting Points

One way to determine the color story for your bouquet is to look to a single flower. A variegated rose of red and white, for instance, can serve as the beginning note for a mix of flowers in various shades of reds, pinks, and whites. Similarly, a dark-centered calla lily can offer a range of colors in a single stem, each subtle shift in hue becoming the inspiration for other flowers that reflect that particular part of the spectrum.

For one particularly elegant wedding, we mixed a lavish, classical selection of PG hydrangeas and garden roses with astilbes, ornamental cabbages, and calla lilies. The rose and hydrangea colors were based on the calla lilies, each of which ranged from pale buttery yellow on the outside of the blossom to orange and to deep wine in the center. We fringed it all with feathery spears of dark red astilbes.

It made for a bouquet perfectly at home at a swank hotel. Though these weddings usually are held in the evening, you can bet this type of bouquet will be carried by the "princess for a day."

A calla lily with a deep burgundy center served as the inspiration for this bouquet's quiet lyrical colors and its contrasting bolder darks. A pale green ornamental cabbage (look closely at the bottom of the bouquet) can almost pass for one of the clustered roses. This is a luscious fall combination almost wild with decadence.

Fiesta Flowers
Joys of Early Fall

To capture the vibrancy of late summer and early fall days, a Mexican sunflower can spark a bright, happy bouquet. Put little yellow mums with buttoned brown centers next to large sunflowers, red dahlias, roses, and sprigs of mint, then jazz it up with tiny vermilion pompons of globe amaranths, merry crashers to the party.

Party? Perhaps fiesta is more appropriate. Mexican sunflowers are special, a step away from the ordinary that you won't see every day, though that may be short-lived as their perky face has lately enjoyed a rise in popularity.

Another fun touch to an early-fall bouquet can be added by blending large sunflowers with smaller mums that have similar coloring and shape, making for a Mama Bear–Baby Bear pairing.

Yellow mum

Dahlia

Globe amaranth

Rose

Mexican sunflower

Sunflower

Mint

The pieces come together: A simple sleeve of solid cloth held by an open French braid of ribbon responds to sister colors among the flowers and underscores the bouquet's festive, casual theme.

Feast for the Eyes
Fruits and Flowers

For centuries, artists from the Dutch masters to the Fauvists have drawn on the natural beauty of flowers and the bountiful succulence of fruit to create still life tours de force. That trend has been recently revived as fruits increasingly find their way into traditional floral arrangements such as centerpieces. Flower markets and farmer's markets sell fruits on branches and vines for decorative purposes; you can also wire fruits that aren't on stems.

It's still relatively rare to see flower and fruit bouquets carried down the aisle, though a single nosegay can tell a fascinating story of nature's cycle: First there's foliage, then the tree bears a flower, which then begets fruit. It's a combination that harkens back to ancient times and celebrates each season with all that season has to offer. Each stage of the plant is beautiful, so look at every one of them, not just the flowers, to find worthy material for a bouquet.

Keep in mind that each piece of fruit can significantly increase the bouquet's weight. You can't spend the day lugging around a crate of oranges. Select fruits that work in harmony with flowers, but leave a faint footprint. Use larger fruits sparingly and, if possible, find mini-versions of your favorites.

Sophisticated and formal, this mix of apricot Camel roses, mini-pomegranates, black chile peppers, hosta leaves, bleeding heart leaves, and hydrangea macrophyllas is well suited to the chic and confident bride.

The stems of this early-autumn bouquet are dressed in materials that complement this lush mix. The wrapping, a vivid burnt sienna jacket tailored to the bouquet, is trimmed with a spine of square buttons.

Hosta leaf

Hydrangea
macrophylla

Mini-pomegranates

Black

Uptown Doyenne

The Asters

Asters derive their name from the Greek word for "star," an appropriate moniker despite the flower's being perceived as a common garden flower. Relatively inexpensive and extremely popular as a flowering plant—there are hundreds of varieties—they have true star power to spare when called to duty for a bouquet. Their appeal is a quiet one, with a beauty that lingers in the mind. As Emerson wrote, "Every aster in my hand/Goes home loaded with a thought."

Asters have a range from snowy white to dark purple, but are often the pinks and reds seen here. These tiny relatives of the sunflower provide a bright

A Fresh Look
Chrysanthemums Rediscovered

Laughter and happiness: That's what chrysanthemums bring a home, according to followers of feng shui. And who's to argue? With countless varieties, sizes, and colors, mums can brighten and enliven almost every type of bouquet.

The strong association of chrysanthemums with homecoming corsages the size of cheerleaders' pompons or dyed-green specials for Saint Patrick's Day makes some people automatically reject these flowers as bouquet choices. Our two cents? These are beautiful flowers. They've been revered for thousands of years in Japan and China; it's time for the western world to drop the taboo and step forward to embrace these densely layered blossoms. It's the same story with carnations, which we've also worked to revitalize as a worthy floral choice, and with the unfairly tarnished cockscomb.

Okay, we have to admit that we, too, were once part of that crowd that pooh-poohed this flower; quite frankly, it sort of spooked us in an Edward Gorey kind of way. But we opened our minds, and our arrangements, to include this velvety plant with an arresting palette. Once we got past ourselves and gave this little trooper a chance, we discovered that it makes great filler. The moral of this long story is that all flowers are beautiful if presented properly, and all flowers deserve consideration. It just proves again how wrong it is to be a snob.

By the way, the terms *mum* and *chrysanthemum* are used interchangeably, though, roughly speaking, mums are chrysanthemums with side shoots pinched so that all the plant's energy is concentrated on just one bloom per stem, which can eventually result in some gargantuan blossoms—see "homecoming corsages" and "dyed-green specials" above!

This bouquet from the heart of fall features a clutch of orange chrysanthemums infused with privet berries, hypernicum berries, and red peppers. The colors are repeated in the elegant two-toned ribbons of the handle.

OPPOSITE: These impish yellow mums, buttoned in brown, are harmony personified. A large brown power bow that matches the flowers' centers catches it all together; a single, perfect blossom plays double duty as a cameo adorning the bow's center.

Basil

Cockscomb

Chrysanthemum

Chrysanthemum

Lysimachia

Western albino cedar

Rippled, velvety cockscombs are tucked among a jamboree of yellows, greens, and burgundies. The cockscombs are used in coordination with Western albino cedar sprigs of almost the same color.

Seasonal Surprise
Autumn's White Bouquet

Sometimes the order of the day is anything but fall colors for an autumn bouquet. No problem; there's a white bouquet for every season, and this one is no exception: dahlias, hydrangeas, roses, snowberry branches—the possibilities are endless.

If you want to give your whites a seasonal flare without resorting to a tired old color lineup, using foliage that bespeaks the season is a good way to go. The dark richness of hosta leaves, for example, gives an autumnal feel to an all-white flower mix, while still letting whites be the center of attention.

And don't forget geography if you're going with an all-white bouquet. Your bouquet may be largely composed of mass-produced flowers from a far-off land—roses, say, or hydrangeas. But nothing looks sillier than a classic English garden–style white posy on the beaches of Jamaica or a formal cascade of snowy white stephanotis blossoms at a backyard BBQ. So, "When in Rome . . . ." Look to your surroundings to key your bouquet. In a tropical setting, for instance, blend in a local flower—an orchid perhaps—for a bouquet tailored to time and place.

Large ruffled hydrangeas, impersonating fine white-on-white toile de Jouy, get cozy with sprigs of freesia boasting columns of blossoms in various stages of bloom. Grounding the bouquet firmly in autumn are the large green hosta leaves that frame the whites.

Spinning Wheels
The Fall Biedermeier Bouquet

Bright yellow, pale lemon, off-white, greens: Ah, the colors of fall.

Yes, fall. Sometimes it's not the color but the floral species that determines a bouquet's seasonal attitude. A yellow-white ornamental cabbage resembling a large tea rose (they're known as cabbage roses for a reason), for example, lets light colors be introduced without worry that the bouquet will read as too summery. Used at the center of a Biedermeier bouquet, as we've done on the one pictured here, this distinctly autumnal nucleus spins the seasonal tone definitively—this is a flower that you can't get at other times of the year!

From that elegant start, we surrounded the center with an octet of pale lemon roses, then segued smoothly to a starburst of pale green foliage surrounded by bright yellow carnations. A bold collar of lamb's ears, slightly overlapping, completed the dance of colors. Once more? Yellow-white cabbage, green edge, lemon yellow roses, pale green foliage, yellow carnations, green leaves. Or, more simply put, yellow-green-yellow-green-yellow-green.

And while such strict constructions were once reserved for the most old-fashioned and prim among us (and we don't mean roses), maintaining a clean, crisp outline in the design sets the bouquet securely in the twenty-first century.

A creamy yellow–white ornamental cabbage edged in dark green holds center stage in this impressive Biedermeier. Sharing the spotlight, a collar of Limoncello spray roses is offset by radiating forsythia leaves, and a plush ring of yellow carnations is capped by a skirt of lamb's ears.

Ablaze
Calla Lilies

"I love fall! I love the colors of fall! Give me fall!"

When a bride comes to us with a request that passionate, we've no choice but to do the lady's bidding. And nothing serves the lust for fall colors like yellow, orange, and red calla lilies summoning visions of an autumn day straight out of central casting: leaves crunching underfoot, hillsides splashed in an intoxicating brew of glorious fall foliage.

Calla lilies have enjoyed a resurgence in popularity during the past few decades, thanks in part to their rediscovery by artists, photographers, and trendsetters. What served as inspirational subject matter for the likes of Diego Rivera and Georgia O'Keeffe has more recently been interpreted by such photographers as Tina Midotti and Robert Mapplethorpe. When Calvin Klein chose them as one of the few decorative elements displayed around his ultra-spare home decor line, they assumed their current reputation as a minimalist flower, something that has only spurred their popularity with arrangements of all types, including wedding bouquets. Their simple lines bring to mind an Old Hollywood, Sunset Boulevard–type decadence, making them good for a formal mix.

Super hardy, calla lilies have plenty of staying power whether your autumn event is cool and crisp or turns out to be more on the humid summer side.

TALL, SLENDER, AND RICH
Long-stemmed flowers

French tulips

Giant calla lilies

Dinner plate dahlias

Phaleonopsis orchids

Miniature cymbidium orchids

These enormous, elegant blossoms accessorize an equally sleek, modern gown. An inch-wide belt of satin shows off the extreme glory of the stems to the fullest. The look is pure Art Deco glamour. 🌹🌹

OPPOSITE: Sunset-hued calla lilies surrounded by burnt orange take their place in a sea of dense reds. Their pronounced stamen is mimicked by slender, waxy red chile peppers that dot the bouquet. A wrap of red satin is accessorized with a slender, two-toned bow of red and orange. The punch of a single oversized button is the cherry on the sundae. 🌹🌹

Unexpected Bounty

Lady Anne Apples

No fruit is more associated with fall than apples; when the harvest basket tips over, this is the first delicacy to roll out. It's apples that people go bobbing for, it's what they dip in caramel, it's the heart of the perfect fall pie. Yet when a bride asks for a harvest theme in her bouquet and we suggest a mix of flowers and apples, we get more sideway looks than nods.

That all changes when we show her the way a sprinkling of Lady Anne apples turns a standard mix of roses, hydrangeas, or other flowers into a surprisingly rich bouquet that thoroughly and definitively establishes a fall theme.

Lady Annes or other varieties of similar size and weight work best; their small size allows them to snuggle nicely among blossoms that are of equal or greater size. (Larger apples would simply be too heavy and too loud.) Still, even these tiny ones add their fair share of weight, so be sure to limit their number. Besides, with their bold prominence, a few go a long way.

These small green-and-red Lady Anne apples look as if they fell from the tree and landed gently in a bed of fall flowers and leaves. An array of Charlotte roses, hydrangea macrophyllas, oak and locust leaves, lamb's ears, and privet berries are complemented by the moss green of the plush velvet ribbon. 🌹🌹

Exotic Jewel
Orchids

Wedding flowers go through so much drama: They're cut, watered, selected, trimmed, shaped, wired, placed, pinned, and wrapped—and that's all before they're even asked to step in for the long haul of being the bride's all-important, all-day accessory.

Ironically, orchids—flowers that look as fragile as eggshells—are one of nature's sturdiest. For starters, they hail from the deepest regions of tropical rain forests where it's hot, hot, hot and conditions are nothing less than brutal. If there's an October heat wave and the chapel's air-conditioning is on the fritz, the groom might wilt (bachelor party details, please!), but these won't.

One advantage of that strength is that they don't need refrigeration—in fact, they don't even like it. That saves on worrying about storage in the hours leading up to the ceremony. In water or out, they last forever. Place them in a bouquet in the morning, and at the stroke of midnight they still wouldn't dream of drooping.

Time was an orchid passed as a true rarity, an exotic treasure imported from a far-off land to coexist with mere mortals. Now you can buy them in pots at Kmart. Still, they continue to carry an air of exoticism and, at least in bouquets, a hefty price. That said, consider that a single stem of some varieties hold up to sixteen blossoms, so the investment may well be worth it. Don't worry about having too many blooms. When the bride has what she needs, she can share the rest with groom and crew—a single small orchid makes an absolutely perfect boutonniere.

Orchids can be mixed with other flowers with great success. Here, Camel roses rest among long-stemmed Safari anthuriums and touches of russet photinia leaves, their color repeating that of the dappled cymbidium orchids. This is one mighty rich combo.

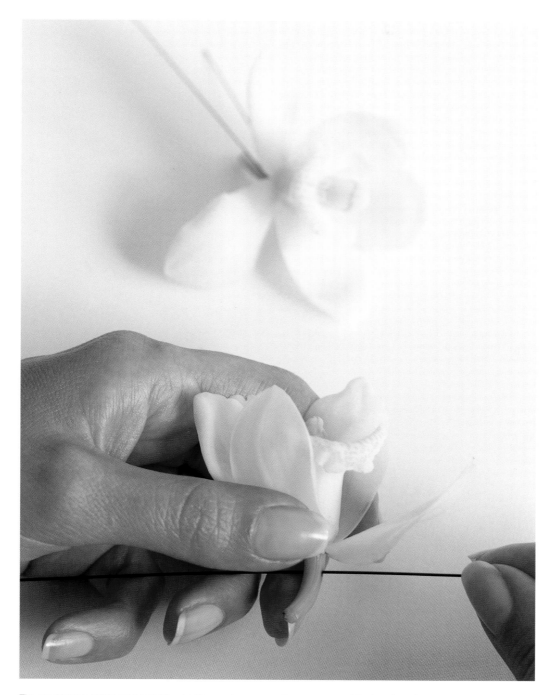

The cymbidium orchid can be easily wired to create a new and more manageable stem to replace its beefy and cumbersome original. We simply threaded a piece of 18-gauge straight wire (available from floral supply or craft stores) through the trimmed stem, directly behind the blossom's head, then bent both sides of the wire down 90 degrees. The result is featherlight and flexible.

OPPOSITE: Phaleonopsis is another orchid only recently available as a cut flower. More delicate than a cymbidium, it provides a natural cascade that is as simple as it is elegant, one perfectly suited for the clean lines of this bridal gown.

Mixed with ferns, the lady slipper orchid's rich hues and distinctive markings evoke a walk through the forest primeval, save for the handle, which sports contrasting ribbon and bow, along with a whimsical pair of tassels. Only recently available as a cut flower, lady slippers have a very expensive look, and rightly so. With only one or two blossoms per plant, this is a pricey selection. 🌹🌹🌹

OPPOSITE: We replaced the thick, heavy stems of yellow cymbidium orchids with wire to create a more manageable handle. Here, about a dozen and a half blossoms are clustered tightly, yet require a handle much slimmer than you might think. An intricately embroidered ribbon of yellows and reds edged in dark tones wraps tightly up the stems, ending in a family jewel of a choker. 🌹🌹

Giving Thanks

Harvest Nosegay

After we get to know a bride and become familiar with what she wants on her wedding day, we can tailor every bit of the wedding design—especially the bouquet—to meet her expectations.

When one of our clients, a back-to-nature bride, described to us her intention to marry her beloved in the middle of a large clearing next to a lake, we knew this was no occasion for a standard arrangement. Though she was as beautiful as any princess, she had no intention of dressing like someone who stepped out of a fairy tale. The planned events included an American Indian blessing, a dinner of wild game, and a lakeside ceremony—where the bride arrived at the altar in a canoe paddled by her brother and accompanied by the family golden lab. Her bouquet needed to reflect a sense of raw nature and untamed beauty. We sprinkled sumptuous flowers with feathers, berries, twigs, tiny fruits, and bold fall leaves.

In short, the Thanksgiving harvest in a nosegay.

History doesn't record the wedding flowers of Captain Smith and Pocahontas, but could her bouquet have more clearly embodied a more sweetly rustic feel than this one? Tangerine roses, ornamental pears, guinea hen feathers, bittersweet berries, twigs, crab apples, and beech leaves: Behold the heart of fall.

Structured Chaos
Fall's Unlikely Juxtapositions

The key to creating a bouquet that's bursting with exuberance but still elegantly presented is to walk a fine line between tightly structured and au naturel free-for-all. Sometimes that can be achieved by careful placement of varieties that on their own seem wild and woolly.

Take the curling Uluhe fiddlehead fern from Hawaii. This beautifully dark plant, which resembles a young purple fiddlehead fern, is almost trippy in its stance, a tiny shepherd's staff of velvet. And consider celosias, fuzzy spears of wild color, shape, and texture. Bring these delicate varieties into a mix of more traditional flowers in classic bouquet forms, as we've done on these pages, and you've transformed an arrangement from staid to stupendous. Long multibladed fern fronds radiate out from the edge, as though the flowers had fallen into the middle of a burst of green fireworks. The fronds are lightweight, so use as many as you need to create the effect you want.

Close examination of the bouquet reveals the prominent role of the Uluhe fiddlehead, which copies the deep wines of the other flowers.

OPPOSITE: This free-for all combination proves that mums can hold their own as a flower of true beauty, even next to the richness of calla lilies, celosias, and Uluhe fiddleheads. The wine-colored leaves are from blueberry bushes.

Surprise Performance
Peonies in Autumn

Peonies, a flower rightly associated with spring, can also make an appearance in the middle of fall. Imports from New Zealand—autumn here, springtime and peonies there—mean the bride can have the flower whenever and wherever she desires. Their dazzling texture, color, and rich beauty are always a joy to behold, particularly when they make a surprise appearance "out of season." The bride who desires extraordinary opulence won't be disappointed. These are the flowers, after all, that have inspired artists for millennia, from scroll painters in ancient China to the alluring still lifes of Renoir.

Another pleasant surprise with peonies is how well they pair with unusual foliage, such as the hypernicum berry leaves, which enrich the peonies' textures and colors.

The imported varieties aren't as lush as those available domestically in season, however, with blossoms a bit skimpier than local springtime specimens. But even though local peonies are a great value in May and June, be ready to pay a pretty penny for these imported guest stars in the fall.

This bouquet has so much depth of color that it appears to have been photographed with infrared. Roses compete with peonies and hypernicum berries and leaves to see which is the deepest red. (This just in: the leaves over the roses in a photo finish!) A boldly striped taffeta ribbon of matching burgundy and contrasting gold completes the scene.

Gray Gardens

Dusty Miller

At that moment in fall when it's too late for zinnias yet too early to trumpet the holidays, it's time to make do with what's available. That might mean looking in places you pass by every single day—including curbside.

That's where you'll find dusty miller, a super hardy gray-leafed plant commonly used as a border on median strips. This low ground cover has a serrated edge and a soft texture that can add an opulent touch to a sophisticated bouquet—just right for the bride who's got it in spades. Used in a mix of light and cheery flowers alongside smoldering deep colors, the gray sets an elegant tone. Yellow mums, for example, can serve as the starting point for a nosegay that flirts between carefree color and serious elements and textures such as dark privet berries and the lustrous gray lavender of dusty miller. Tiny spurts of yellow solidaster can liven the ensemble.

A bride in platinum gray—even black, which some brides choose as the ultimate elegant statement—could easily be matched to this bouquet.

Throw off unnecessary restrictions when you have to find inspiration; it might be closer than you think. Here it's the gray leaves of dusty miller, a common garden annual, which act as a bridge between serious dark purple thistle heads and capricious sprigs of tiny and large yellow chrysanthemums.

I've Got You, Babe
Hippie Fun and Free

Yes it's hippie, and yes it's one part tutti and two parts fruitti, but so what? If you're a fun, cool, hip (yes, as in hippie) couple, why not go for a love combo of colors in a bouquet to fit you and your daytime outdoor wedding in the country?

When a bride who was to be married in such an affair near Santa Fe approached us with ideas for her ceremony, we responded by creating a peace, love, and happiness bouquet that would be prized at the finest of communes. We began with outrageously bright sunflowers and black-eyed Susans, then tricked it out with stabs of ornamental grasses and even feathers. Can you feel the good vibrations?

As bright and dazzling as our creation was, however, it was also a serious endeavor. For the handle we included a beaded wrap of indigenous art, perfectly suited for this solemn, life-affirming ceremony.

A giant sunflower is surrounded by the makings of a very playful bouquet.

CLOCKWISE FROM TOP CENTER: Persian carpet zinnia, black-eyed Susan, zinnia, mini-black-eyed Susans, coin grass, crocosmia, feathers, and another Persian carpet zinnia. A beaded fringe the bride-to-be bought on a trip to New Mexico will serve as the handle's ornamentation.

OPPOSITE: Bright yellow field flowers vie for attention with pheasant feathers and ornamental grasses, all tied together on the stems with a piece of indigenous art.

My Fair Lady
Alstroemeria

The lily, carnation, alstroemeria, and baby's breath: Four lovely flowers, but bunch them together on a restaurant table in a small white vase and the presentation alone turns beauty into gaudy.

Don't blame the flowers. A poet once wrote about "the touch of the master's hand," in which a dusty old violin was being auctioned for "one dollar, two dollars, who'll give me three?" when an old gentleman approached the auction table, tuned the violin, and proceeded to play an entrancing concerto. When he finished, the crowd burst into applause and the auctioneer resumed, "One thousand, two thousand, who'll give me three?"

To bring out the full beauty of flowers, especially common varieties, play them to their fullest natural advantage.

Suffragettes used to say, "A common woman is as common as a loaf of bread, and she will rise!" We nominate all those "common" flowers"—the carnation, the lily, baby's breath, and the supermarket variety alstroemeria— as candidates up to the task of being great.

The alstromeria in particular. Sometimes called the Peruvian lily or lily-of-the-Incas, it is a little-used true beauty and deserves to be in the top echelon of flowers, thanks to its fine detail and butterfly petals.

Its beautiful nature comes with a hardy soul. No matter how long the day, how tightly gripped, how glaring and hot the photographer's lights, this flower will soldier on.

For a bouquet of very uncommon alstroemerias, the stem treatment's colors put the cherry on the sundae: A banana-colored jacket of starched linen is stitched with dark brown thread; together the two colors mimic the markings of the flower in a color combination that says autumn is here. 🌹

Firecracker

Red, White . . . and Fall

Red and white is typically associated with summer—picnic blankets, beach umbrellas, sporty convertibles—but autumn brims with these colors, too. And although rarely a wedding duo, for the right kind of party—an Indian summer picnic perhaps—this is a crackling combo.

For the white part, fluffy white chamomiles (they resemble small mums) and andromeda bells, with their drooping clusters of fragrant, bell-like blossoms and brilliant, glossy, dark leaves, are two excellent choices. But there's one little blossom that's the true star of autumn whites, and not just for its shape: The wax flower requires only the brief light of shortened days in order to begin budding, making it a seasonal specialty.

As for the reds: Few are as rich, vivid, and hot as the leaves of the burning bush. The name alone tells you this is a very bold hue that embodies all of the heat of the season. During spring and summer, burning bush—also known as cork tree—has leaves of dark green, but the cool nights of autumn turn it to a red that nearly glows.

Fiery leaves of burning bush flicker among buttons of white chamomile, white-tipped red dahlias, white sprigs of andromeda bells, and spikes of freesia. Tiny clusters of white wax flowers, with their simple childlike flower shape, enliven the mix.

Andromeda bells

Freesia

Wax flowers

Dahlia

Burning bush foliage

Chamomile

Sugar and Nice
Flower Girl Bouquet

Mention to friends that you're considering carnations as a wedding flower and don't be surprised if you raise an eyebrow or two. As one of the most cost-efficient and long-lasting flowers available, carnations have been saddled with the reputation as an inexpensive (horrors!) and common (double horrors!) selection.

Yet beyond the unfair public perceptions is a flower with a soft luster, gentle fragrance, and joyous color palette all rolled inside a thicket of fringed petals that epitomize chic femininity. This is the blossom, after all, whose Latin name is *dianthus,* which translates to "divine flower."

Pink carnations are a particularly sweet choice for a bouquet, but one that must be approached with a bit of restraint. So sweet is this selection that it's almost too much for an adult. Instead, consider how to translate that sugary appeal into a more appropriate venue, such as the flower girl bouquet.

Get ready for a sugar rush with this cotton candy–pink carnation bouquet, bound by a pink gingham wrap with felt-embroidered buttons, and streaming long trails of bright pink ribbon. Its endearing sweetness makes it perfect for the flower girl.

Winter

Is there anything more tranquil and reassuring than the light of a winter morning, the quiet blaze of color that introduces the day? It's a moment that proves the fallacy that winter is gray and lifeless. It may be the end of the life cycle, but just as every day holds light, winter holds the promise of spring.

It's also a season of celebration with family and friends, renewing old acquaintances, sharing and giving, enjoying togetherness with comfort food, hot toddies, and snuggling in front of the fireplace.

From hushed palettes to eye-popping greens, reds, and blues to gold and silver, winter colors laugh at the cold. It's an ebullient and inspiring time.

Ironically, in a season that expects no flowers to bloom, every flower is appropriate. It's a floral paradox that allows imports from hothouses and the far corners of the world, such as orchids, tulips, and daffodils, to step out of spring and find a home in a winter bouquet.

Adding to the festivity are the tokens of the season—red berries, tiny pinecones, sprigs of spruce, cranberries, a silver bell, a fluff of marabou— that bring a wintry touch to the most tropical bloom.

It's a season for revelry and joy and celebrations of the spirit that lie within.

A series of small pomanders dangles from strands of faux pearls. The pale blue ribbon and cluster of oversized "gems" fix the bow just below the wrist. We've held the flowers—tiny white mums—to the form with tiny pearl head pins, giving the pomanders a special luster. 🌹🌹🌹

World on a String
Pomanders

Back when Louis XIV was calling the shots, pomanders were the ball of the belle. They've never quite had that same allure since. Still, the style is a fascinating, albeit unorthodox, one—a perfect sphere of flowers—and, under the right circumstances, it can make a delightful splash.

When placed around the arm, the handle makes a foolproof carrier, a good option for very young flower girls who might benefit from one less thing to worry about as they walk down the aisle.

Pomanders are also possible options for the bride herself: if she's escorted down the aisle by both parents, say, and wants to keep her hands free, or if she wants to carry only a prayer book in her hands but still wants to have flowers.

Whatever flower is used, these deceptively simple bouquets require a few special techniques to build, and a lot more flowers than you might expect; the pomander pictured here contains approximately 250 blooms—in other words, it isn't for the budget conscious.

Although a pomander is expensive because of the sheer quantity of flowers used, making one is a pretty easy proposition. A small Styrofoam ball, available at any craft or floral supply store, becomes the armature for the multitude of blossoms; the stems have been snipped and replaced with wire so that they can be inserted into the ball more easily. Packed as densely as possible, the flowers turn into a plush snowball. No throwing, please!

POMANDER POWER
Ideal flowers

Chrysanthemums

Roses

Spray roses

Small dahlias

Stephanotis blossoms

Cymbidium orchids

Marigolds

Craspedias

Gomphrenas

Mini-carnations

Approximately 250 Viviane spray rose blossoms are employed to create the minimalist form of this pomander. The "purse strings" are fashioned from green organdy ribbon. The glint of an antique broach seals the deal. ❀❀❀

December Bride

Holiday Reds

Winter is a season of cozy plaids, bright blue, gold, and silver. The palette stirs warm thoughts of the very spirit of the holidays—family and friends, giving, peace, and love. But it's the color red that truly reflects the season's holiday warmth and joy and the bountiful ways we express them. In any other season, red is just . . . well, red. But come wintertime, red means Christmas, all the time. It's the very symbol of Christmas, from Santa's suit to the cheeks of holiday carolers.

So be advised: If your wedding is planned for December and you don't want to be a "Christmas bride," avoid red.

On the other hand, if you're looking for a celebration that reflects the spirit of the holiday, use the color in every way you can: Flowers, sure, but also red velvet, cranberries, peppermint swirls. If you decide to go for it, you might as well go all the way.

LEFT: This wedding's flower theme begins with the boutonniere, a snip of tartan ribbon pinned to a sprig of spruce and berries.

RIGHT: The bridesmaids will each carry a single element of the bride's bouquet, starting with (clockwise from top left) bouquets of tulips, roses, anemones, and red ilex berries, each tied with the signature plaid ribbon.

Oodles of red roses, tulips, and anemones somehow make room for even more red in the form of red ilex berries on tiny branches. Cranberries are strung together for the trails that stream from a tartan plaid handle. This bouquet embraces the holiday spirit with so much exuberance and variety of elements that it can easily be deconstructed to create special single-specimen bouquets for the four bridesmaids, each specimen successfully standing on its own, spreading its own brand of holiday cheer. 🌹🌹🌹

Ice Princess

Inspired by Fashion

To make a bouquet reflect the season, think of things that *are* the season. Fur muffs, jingle bells, ice-skating—they're all inspirations when you're wondering where to begin.

For a bride who chose Aspen in winter for her wedding, we decorated her bouquet with puffs of ski-bunny fur. For a bride who planned a rustic party at a Rocky Mountain cabin in Idaho, we accessorized with buffalo plaid.

The location not only sets the tone, it often provides the ingredients as well. Tiny pinecones, bright berries—these gifts of nature fit so well with winter designs because they are themselves the very nature of the season.

Add to that the iconic clothing of winter, from fur muffs to pompon hats to woolly plaids, and you've got tons of ideas for accessorizing your bouquet with the season's best finery.

An ice-blue collar of marabou snuggles up beneath a flurry of white alliums and pale blue tweedias, an ensemble fashionable enough for a Saint Moritz chalet or a spin around the rink at Rockefeller Center. Tassels of silver bells front a white satin wrap that lets stems peek out from below, adding a touch of extra color to this refined creation.

Single Note
Anemones

A simple, modern gown requires elegant but understated flowers. One easy solution is a bouquet made from a single variety, and one good choice is the lush, brightly colored anemone. (This kind of bouquet can be a bit too austere with a plain Jane flower.)

Anemones are a spring flower, but they're a little wimpy in the heat, which tends to turn them inside out. They work best when there is a nip in the air. If you can afford them as imports—not surprisingly, they're on the costly side—consider bringing them into your winter mix.

With a one-variety bouquet, where there are only two or three elements, the ribbon and trim take on increased importance. Choose a ribbon that coordinates not only with the flower but also with the gown. A sleek, straight-line dress, for example, calls for a ribbon that reflects its texture and sensuousness.

AN ECHO OF ITSELF: Flowers to use solo, available by season

Spring: Tulips, parrot tulips, peonies, French anemones, daffodils, ranunculus, lilies of the valley, sweet peas, pansies, garden roses, blossoming trees (lilac, azalea, cherry, crab apple), snowballs

Summer: Marguerite daisies, dahlias, sunflowers, delphiniums, roses

Autumn: Dahlias, sunflowers, roses, chrysanthemums, amaryllises

Winter and year-round: Stephanotis, mini-calla lilies, cymbidium orchids, lady's slipper orchids, cattlea orchids, alstroemerias, carnations and mini-carnations, gypsofilas, Hanna asters, roses

An intensely hued satin ribbon contrasts dramatically with the gown's opulent whiteness, yet it reflects its texture and sensuousness. The ribbon also plays well against the magenta anemones, exactly copying the color of their rich, deep centers.

Everyday Holiday
Amaryllises

Amaryllis is one showy flower, and that's not even counting what it looks like in a bouquet. Growing on leafless stalks of up to a half-yard tall, with each stem producing several enormous trumpet blossoms of white, off-white, peach, pink, or red, amaryllis is a stunning flower straight from the garden. Now, imagine it in a bouquet.

Red amaryllises are very popular during the winter, when they serve as mainstays on holiday tables or as gifts as potted plants. But that seasonal attachment shouldn't preclude the species from stepping beyond Christmas. All that's needed is a presentation that includes colors, textures, and additional floral materials that channel other moods. Why not pair it with tropical foliage and grasses, for instance—the perfect mix for a ceremony on the beach at Waikiki. This is one flexible flower that looks equally at home as the center of a holiday display or in a romantic bouquet fit for a princess.

Amaryllis stems, as big as a broom handle and hollow as a straw, draw up large reserves of water after cutting. Even at weddings that go from morning to night, expect the flower to look good regardless of how late the hour.

There's no need to shout, especially when the bride wants to project restrained elegance. This is a bouquet filled with sumptuous pinks and whites, but punctuation marks of dark privet berries keep the blushing pink amaryllises and two softly hued varieties of roses from coming off too sweet. Thin trails of two-toned ribbon project a similarly reserved air, offering a touch of grace but no competition from the dress. 🌹🌹

OPPOSITE: Candy-colored amaryllises, in various stages of bloom, provide so much wattage that they benefit from the quieting effect of gray leucodendron berries. The tiny, red berrylike dots are actually unopened buds of the wax flower. A fabric wrap of red-and-white toile de Jouy continues the color theme and establishes the formal, traditional nature of this bouquet. But it is the holidays, after all, so a string of cranberry trails is most welcome. 🌹🌹

A passel of pale white-green amaryllises
makes a lovely sheath when the tail end
of autumn is indiscernible from the icy
beginnings of winter. Paired with long
white spears of andromeda bells, dainty
hellebores, and trickling blades of deep
green liriope leaves trimmed in white,
this bouquet reads anything but holiday.
Our smooth green handle resembles a
swath of satin but, in fact, is a single
large tropical leaf (available from tropical
flower supply stores) wrapped tightly
around the stems. Several strands of
deep green liriope leaves knot into the
bow. 🌹🌹🌹

Biker Chic

Baby's Breath

The delicate fragrance and petite bloom of baby's breath is how this lovely little flower got its name, but that's probably the last time anyone has said a nice word about it. After years of playing garish second fiddle in bouquets—kind of like a gangly plug of parsley next to the main course—baby's breath is slowly shaking its status as a flower unworthy of consideration as a central player.

In fact, we think baby's breath is perfectly suitable as the main course itself, and offer it as an example of how something can become special if it's treated right. An ideal opportunity to put forward this notion came when a client, a self-described "biker chick," asked us to create something befitting her lifestyle. This was a bride who derived a bit of glee each time she poked the Establishment in the eye, and she was damned if her bouquet would be anything à la Stepford.

We agreed that she would look silly carting a big, flouncy posy down the aisle. So we went with the streamlined profile of baby's breath all by itself. We then harnessed it in leather and trimmed it in hardware. The result was a bouquet that was as lively and individual as our bride. Mission accomplished!

A trim white leather sleeve, cinched with a tiny black leather belt studded with metal loops, redefines this humble cloud of baby's breath as the utmost in cool. 🌿

Puttin' on the Ritz

Stephanotis

When a bride-to-be asks for stephanotis, it's clear that hers will be a tiptop affair. Sometimes referred to as Madagascar jasmine, stephanotis originated in Madagascar and was first introduced to England in the beginning of the nineteenth century. Ever since, this fragrant, delicate, and expensive bloom has been the signature for traditional and formal weddings the world over. And why not? Some of the most revered icons of style—Jacqueline Kennedy, Princess Diana, even Audrey Hepburn—chose stephanotis to accompany them down the aisle. If it was good enough for this tony trio . . .

The stephanotis—actually an evergreen climbing shrub with long tendrils and glossy green leaves—sprouts pure white blossoms from a thin curling vine. The blossoms arrive in the market stem-free and are sold in packages, presented like an elegant box of white chocolates. Florists wire the blooms, creating their own "stems" so they can work the flowers into their creations, either as elegant, cascading chains or simply as a feature in a traditional nosegay or sheath. Pearl head pins are often used to hold them in place in a bouquet or, when the bouquets are strung together in rows, to cap the end of the wires.

Stephanotis is perfect for a wedding any time of year, but is especially nice in winter, when its snowy white perfection mirrors the chill in the air.

Lei-like trails of stephanotis, each finished with a teardrop pearl, hang beneath a mix of amaryllises and stephanotis. The pearls add beauty and finesse, but they also serve as caps to hold the rows of stephanotis in place on wires. This is a spectacular formal bouquet worthy of a royal wedding. Fittingly, our princess bride is wearing a classic full dress awash in satin and brocade. 🌹🌹🌹🌹

OPPOSITE: These prim, starched collars, which look as though they were pulled directly from a Franz Hals painting, encircle a snow dome of fragrant white; at the center of each star-shaped blossom is an icy pearl-tipped pin, and folded beneath are velvety white tulips. The whole presentation's relatively small footprint only serves to underscore its dainty exquisiteness. 🌹🌹🌹

Lara's Bouquet
Beyond Christmas

Cedar, juniper, berries—these are elements closely associated with December holidays, but there is a simple way of incorporating them into a winter arrangement without telegraphing Christmas: Stay away from colors and flowers that convey a holiday message, such as amaryllises, roses, and tulips in the signature reds of the holiday. Instead, pair the evergreens of winter— perhaps with an appropriately colored velvet ribbon—with contrasting flowers of spring, such as daffodils or paper whites. Funny enough, when the weather outside is frightful, the flower market starts to wake up from its winter sleep long before the season actually ends, juxtaposing the foliages and berries of the winter landscape with optimistic bundles of spring culled from hothouses around the world.

Why not take inspiration from the market? The effect will be as though a spring bouquet magically pushed through the snow. It's hard not to think of Dr. Zhivago, embracing winter but promising tomorrow ("Someday, my love, whenever the spring breaks through . . ."). You almost expect Lara to appear.

Juniper leaves and their berries play among snow-white tulips and clusters of paperwhites containing a tiny kiss of yellow in their centers. The matte sheen of the berries is carried through in ruffles of dusty miller. A plush green velvet ribbon wraps the handle studded with a line of white pearl buttons. The stems of varying colors confirm the natural winter feel of the bouquet.

Nutcracker Sweet

Spring Visits Winter

It's the middle of winter, yet by filling a bouquet with the very essence of spring and summer—ranunculus, narcissuses, pale roses—it's easy to turn back the calendar to evoke thoughts of warmer days. It's a bouquet that mimics real life, when a late February day has the look of winter while at the same time offering hints of spring.

To make the springtime flowers fit in with the winter spirit, toss in nuts and tiny pinecones. Simply attach wires to them and place them in the bouquet as if they were flowers. Delicate branches of fir and cedar make for beautiful winter reminders, too. A sprinkling of unshelled almonds, Brazil nuts, and pecans in the bouquet brings to mind the beloved holiday tale of the Nutcracker, with delicate Clara frolicking in the land of dancing snowflakes and sugar plum fairies with her wondrous Nutcracker prince.

Wintertime is also underscored by little flourishes of evergreen, boughs that may only recently have held fragile dustings of snow. Yet by spicing the bouquet with sunny yellow flowers, spring is playfully added.

If the bouquet leaves you wondering if it's spring or winter outside, consider the arrangement a successful bridge between the seasons, kind of like seeing a robin on a snowbank.

FOLLOWING PAGES: Spruces, cedars, and eucalyptus berries nestle in a bevy of spring yellows—roses, ranunculus, and avalanche narcissuses—and the deep browns of smoke bush leaves, clusters of wired nuts, and pinecones. A ray of hope and warmth, this bouquet shouts, "Spring is on its way!"

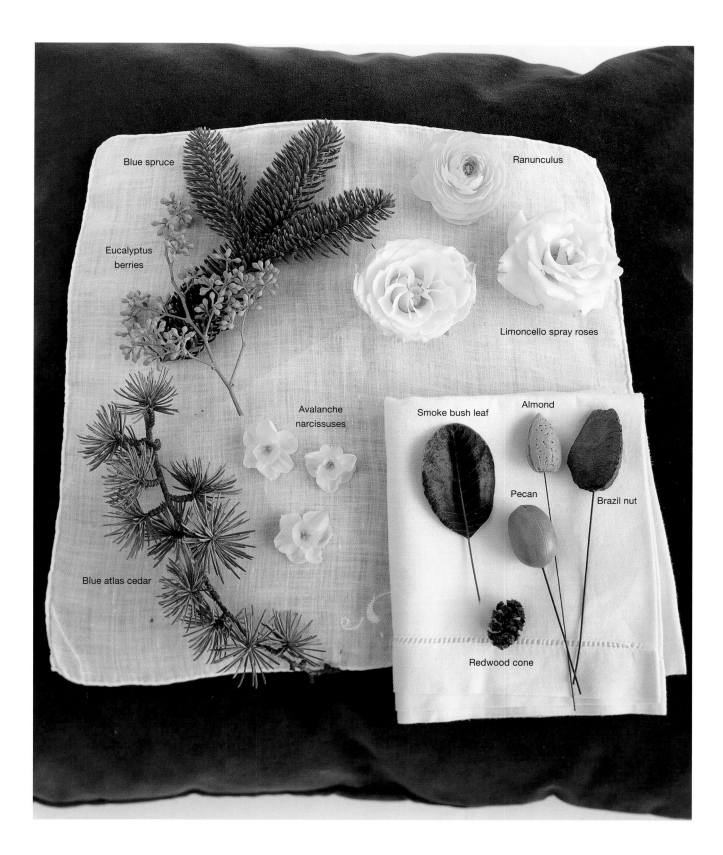

Blue spruce

Ranunculus

Eucalyptus
berries

Limoncello spray roses

Avalanche
narcissuses

Smoke bush leaf

Almond

Pecan

Brazil nut

Blue atlas cedar

Redwood cone

Fiery Glamour
Mimosa

The flowers and foliage of the mimosa tree constitute some of the most amazing of nature's floral offerings. Brilliantly fragranced, these yellow-green flowers, native to Australia, were imported to the Mediterranean regions of Europe in the mid-nineteenth century. A popular roadside planting, they are now among the area's most common flowers.

In many parts of Europe, especially Italy, this is a flower given on Festa della Donna (Women's Day), and it is so strongly identified with that holiday that it rarely has the opportunity to step out and shine for other occasions. Like other flowers casually stigmatized, we love it and use it and do so with pleasure, but it remains exotic here, and rarely is the connection made between brunch's favorite cocktail and the source of its elegant name.

When mimosa flowers brilliant yellow, blossoms akin to pompons fill whole branches with glowing light. Before they open, however, the buds are tightly packed, bright yellow beads, with hundreds on a single branch, beautiful in their own right. The moral of this story is that all stages of a flower can offer beautiful possibilities, so when you're selecting a flower, think beyond the blossom to achieve the look you desire.

This extravagant winter bouquet, with bold red amaryllises cushioned by mini-showers of young mimosa buds, sparks with unconventional glamour. 🌹🌹

To Preserve and Protect Bouquets

A variety of flower-preserving methods offers varying degrees of success. If you want to try one yourself, be sure to practice on other flowers first before you attempt your wedding bouquet.

Microwaving is at the helm of new technology used by preservation specialists, but different flowers require different drying times, and microwaves can be hazardous if not used properly (think *Gremlins)*, so be careful. This may be something you'd best leave to professionals. Your florist should be able to arrange the connection or look online. The finished product is uncanny, with the bouquet forever frozen in its original state and ready for a shadow box or glass dome.

A less radical approach is glycerin, which replaces the water in the stems, leaves, and petals and preserves the flowers from within. Put the flowers in a vase containing two parts warm water and one part glycerin. Expect mixed results.

Fresh blossoms can also be dried by completely surrounding them with fine, clean sand or silica gel (actually a sandlike powder). In an airtight container, pour a deep layer of sand and place the flowers face up within. Gently pour additional sand all around, on and in each blossom until they're totally covered. Place the lid on the container and allow to dry for two weeks or so; the sand will withdraw moisture while simultaneously supporting the shape. Household mixtures of cornstarch and cornmeal work the same way.

For the less energetic, there's air drying. Loosely hang flowers upside down in a dark, dry, warm area for two to three weeks.

The simplest way to save a flower is by pressing it between the pages of a heavy book. This works best on flatter flowers—pansies and daisies, for example—or smaller versions of more rotund blossoms, such as tiny rosebuds. Flatten while the flower still has its shape and color. Dried out and a bit faded, the cherished souvenirs can then be scrapbooked or framed behind glass. Simply leaving them in the book works, too—you could do worse than to be flipping through your big dictionary twenty years from now and come across a single stem from your wedding bouquet tucked discreetly between *journey* and *joy.*

Acknowledgments

I am very fortunate to collaborate (daily!) with some of the most talented people far and wide, and truly, a project like *To Have & To Hold* could not have been possible without the genius, dedication, and sheer artistry of this team. Susie Montagna, the floral wizard behind my curtain, is just as responsible for the birth of this book as I am. Her finely tuned eye, her attention to detail, and her unbelievable talents—not just with flowers but with anything she touches—is a treasured resource to me and to everyone at our event planning firm. Avi Adler, my cherished comrade and partner in all of our design work, this book is just as much yours as it is mine, and I thank you from the bottom of my heart.

I am blessed to have both a brilliant poet and pal in John Morse, who toiled in my kitchen with such unwavering dedication and good cheer, transforming the common stew of my plain Jane words into an exquisite feast of gourmet prose. Thank you, John. I see this book as yours, too, and could never have done this without you.

Of course, there are many other talented folks that I must single out. Natie Gutierrez's magic touch is on every single bouquet in this book, and Mick Hales's elegant, sumptuous photographs of

Thank you, Mom and Dad. Both you and your marriage continue to be a great inspiration to me.

—David

our work could not be more luscious—you can practically smell the flowers! Thank you, Mick, for going above and beyond for us.

The gowns within these pages, by the most talented designers in the industry—Vera Wang, Angel Sanchez, Wearkstatt, and Reem Akra—certainly established our mission from the outset, inspiring us to fashion bouquets worthy of their dreamy designs.

Many thanks to each of you as well as to Mark Ingram of New York City's unrivaled Bridal Atelier, who was so generous in providing us with many of the gowns that you see throughout these pages.

The incredible yellow-and-white daisy cake on page 110 was made especially for this book by one of the most talented confection artists we've ever worked with. Thank you, Cheryl Kleinman, for your mouthwatering contribution to our story.

I am so lucky to often work on our events with two talented photographers, Philippe Cheng and Kathy Litwin, who were both kind enough to open their archives of photographs to us, one stunning wedding after another. Their images, taken at real weddings, are proof positive that fantasy can become reality, and I thank them both for years of wonderful event collaborations and for gracing our pages with their work.

We are proud to call Artisan home and to be adopted by a publishing house that creates the most elegant books around. This is a house where the family members *love* books, love the process of creating books, and go to work every day with the intention of making *art*. I am thrilled to be surrounded by people who care about those kinds of things. Big

thank-yous to Ann Bramson, Laurie Orseck, and Ellice Goldstein for watering our garden with such love, and to Pamela Cannon, as well, for although we did not finish the project together, it was you who bought the seeds! Vivian Ghazarian and Mark Lerner did such a beautiful job of designing *To Have & To Hold*, and anyone that knows me knows just how hard it is for me to take a leap of faith in that arena, especially my fabulous agent, Carla Glasser. Thank you, Carla, for always taking such good care of me, fighting for what I believe in, doing it with such honesty and good spirit, and for bringing me to the fine folks at Artisan.

And yes, it takes a village. There are many, many people at our event planning concern that work very hard, are unbelievably creative, and are collaborators on everything we do; I must take the opportunity to mention them all since this book would not have been possible without their many varied talents: Jennifer Goebel, our incredible general manager and my prized partner in crime, Charo Figueroa, Marco Mendez, Roy Schofer, Michele Woods, Meg Gleason, Donna Estes, Michelle Mutter, Niki Eways, Lindsay Rubin, Incia Pleytez, Caroline Wolfe, Anne Feve Jones, Meg Gleason, Juliana Jaramillo, Siri Warren, Susie Montagna, Natie Gutierrez, Alissa Reynolds, Maricruz Anzures, Dana Rosen, Karena Bullock, Corrie Hogg, Ariane Triay, Elaina Pennola—you guys rock!

And last but not least, another big thank-you to my business partner, Avi Adler. It's been a wonderful journey.

—David Stark